Front cover

Midwinter solstice sunset, snow in foreground

STONEHENGE EXPERIENCE

- a guide through millennia of building monument and legend.

By Carol Druce

Table of Contents

PART ONE - Before Stonehenge

Prehistoric British Landscape
Mesolithic Post Holes
Causewayed Enclosures
Long Barrows
The Heel Stone
Cursus

PART TWO - Building the Monument

The Henge c.3,000 BC
Station Stones
Aubrey Holes
Bluestones c.2,920 - 2,550 BC
Sarsen Phase 2,660 BC onwards
Durrington Walls 2,660 - 2,600 BC
Preparing the Sarsens
Sarsen Trilithons
Raising the Sarsen Stones
Sarsen Circle
Micaceous Sandstone/Altar Stone
Entrance
Removal of Stations Stones
Rearrangement of Bluestones
Astronomical Alignments
Rituals
Life at Durrington Walls
Woodhenge
Cuckoo Stone
Bronze Age Burial Mounds 2,500 BC
Carvings
The Avenue 1,900 BC

Y and Z Holes
A Few Last Thoughts…

PART THREE - Legendary Stonehenge

The Greeks
Iron Age 800 BC - 43AD
The Druids
The Romans
The Saxons
Eleventh Century
Twelfth Century
The Legend
Thirteenth Century
Fourteenth - Sixteenth Centuries
Seventeenth Century
Eighteenth Century
Nineteenth Century
Twentieth Century
Twenty First Century
Passing on Knowledge

PART FOUR - Experiencing Stonehenge

Portable Information
Why Here?
Today

The gods did not reveal, from the beginning,
All things to us; but in the course of time,
Through seeking we may learn, and know things better
These things are, we conjecture, like the truth.

But as for certain truth, no man has known it,
Nor will he know it, neither of the gods,
Nor yet of all things of which I speak.
And even if perchance he were to utter
The final truth, he would himself not know it;
For all is but a woven web of guesses.
— XENOPHANES

Father Hesper, Father Hesper, Watch,
Watch night and day
Lest the old wounds of the world be healed,
The glory unsealed.
The golden apple stolen away,
And the ancient secret revealed.
— ALFRED, LORD TENNYSON

Shrine of an unknown God! Strong in decay
Enshrouded lie beneath thy buried past;
Until the wisdom of a wiser day
Reveal the secret of thy stones at last.
— G.W.

What is Stonehenge? It is the roofless past
Man's ruinous myth; his uninterred adoring
Of the unknown sunrise cold and red;
His quest of stars that arch his doomed exploring.

And what is Time but shadows that were cast
By these storm-sculptured stones while centuries fled?
The stones remain; their stillness can outlast
The skies of history hurrying overhead.
— WILLIAM BLAKE

PART ONE

Before Stonehenge

Prehistoric British Landscape

Palaeolithic 2,600,000 - 10,000 BC
Mesolithic 10,000 - 4,000 BC
Early Neolithic 4,000 - 3,400 BC
Middle Neolithic 3,400 - 3,000 BC
Late Neolithic 3,000 - 2,500 BC

About 80 million years ago, Britain was nearer the equator, subsequently it was a great deal warmer than now. Its southern coastline was a hundred kilometres further north of its present location, so sea covered the area that is now southern England. When the prehistoric fish and sea creatures died, they sank to the sea bed where they decayed. The breakdown process continued over tens of thousands of years until the calcium in the animals' bodies was reduced down to chalk, a soft rock. The sea pattern changed leaving land where there had been sea. Silica-rich components of the animals' bodies formed nodules of hard rock called flint which occurs in the chalk. These sometimes contain fossils. The area now known as Salisbury Plain has about 40% of the chalk downland in this country. Flint was used to make tools throughout the stone ages - the Palaeolithic, (about ninety-nine percent of human history), Mesolithic and Neolithic. Flints occur on the surface but the best flint has to be mined for - sometimes a few inches, sometimes several feet into the ground. Flint mines have been discovered locally and artefacts made from the flint of Salisbury Plain have been found all over the country. It was a valuable resource.

Copper Age Chalcolithic 2,500 - 2,200 BC

Copper ore can be found close to the earth's surface, as malachite. It may have been brought to Salisbury Plain from Cornwall. The ore is crushed to powder, heated and the chemical reaction that occurs produces the metal, which can in turn be heated and shaped. A copper axe, although soft and easier to blunt, is lighter and easier to use than a stone one. It enabled the cutting of thicker trees than previously done with flint axes. Before the use of copper tools, timber structures were largely comprised of trees no more than 30 cm in diameter. Copper tools enabled people to cut down timbers up to a meter across.

Early Bronze Age 2,200 - 1,600 BC
Middle Bronze Age   1,600 - 1,200 BC
Late Bronze Age 1,200 - 750 BC

The discovery of adding tin to copper to make bronze resulted in the ability to make tools that were much harder and more durable. Tin was mined in Cornwall, which is why it is reasonable to suppose it was already an existing source for copper.

The scant population of Britain at the beginning of the Palaeolithic were hunter-gatherers who, over generations, had come across Europe and over dry land where the English Channel is today. They searched for wild cereal crops, which they gathered at harvest time and trailed wild animals, which they relied on for food and clothing. They were not Homo sapiens, like us, but earlier human species, *Homo habilis, Homo erectus* and *Homo neanderthalensis*. They lived in close-knit family groups. They made shelters and fires. They made tools such as axes from flint, wood and bone which they used to hunt animals. When the glacial periods of the Ice Age came and ice sheets covered Britain, they suffered periods of extreme cold and prolonged darkness and these hostile conditions meant both people and animals could only live here during interglacial periods, times when the Earth had warmed and thawed. Neanderthals were shorter than their predecessors which helped them withstand the cold. Despite this environment, it was during the depths of the Ice Age about 40,000 years ago that modern humans, *Homo sapiens*, began to appear. There is very little evidence of them in this country apart from the tools they made. Their shelters, clothing and possessions - things like baskets they used to collect food in - were made of natural fibres that do not survive any more than the stories they told around their night fires. Even the landscape they knew has changed dramatically, carved by harsh conditions of ice and frost.

During the last glacial period, 12,500 and 10,500 BC, there was a thaw followed by a deep freeze which came so suddenly that in Northern Europe animals have been found frozen with the contents of their last meal undigested. Volcanoes spewed forth fire and bituminous rain, darkening the sky, blotting the sun, ageing it. In Britain at this time, ice reached south as far as the Thames Valley, beyond which was a tundra, the ground constantly frozen beneath top soil which was itself frozen for much of the year. Vegetation would have been sparse. By the time the Ice Age was coming to a close, dust, known as 'loess', was blown across from Europe and provided the soil for vegetation to grow in, such as birch and pine. By 10,000 BC, juniper was growing on the tundra and dominated the landscape for 1,000 years, by which time hazel, oak and elm were also appearing. A river ran through this landscape, from the north of the tundra, carving a valley out towards the coast. The river valley was very fertile and conducive to growing a variety of edible plants. West of it, forty miles inland of the present coastline, was - unusually - an open area clear of trees comprising wild grasses on chalk downland. This area is now known of as Salisbury Plain.

Annual freezing and thawing of the ground around 10,500 BC had, in a localised area to the west of the river, resulted in gullies created on the slopes of the chalk downland. Additionally the ground became pock-marked with cracks and hollows and in places these periglacial processes left linear banks of chalk known as soil stripes. By 8,000 BC these processes had largely stopped with accumulations of flint nodules and sarsen, (fossilised sandstone), boulders being left on the surface. These boulders were shaped by natural weathering over time creating irregular blocks, some pitted with holes in the surface said by geologists to have been caused where palm roots grew before the rock formed; palms that grew in the tropical prehistoric British climate millions of years ago.

People were nomadic hunter-gatherers. As well as wild cereal grains, they also gathered such seasonal fayre as hazelnuts, dogwood fruit, wild strawberry, hawthorn fruit, and probably tubers and fungi. They hunted for wild animals. Although there was still a land bridge linking Britain to Europe, they could also cross expanses of water by boat and were also skilled seafarers, navigators and astronomers who could plot their way by the stars. People gradually forged inland guided by the river - perhaps returning to an area known since before the last glacial period and which had remained in oral tradition or genetic memory or both. Most of the areas either side of the river were heavily wooded.

Following the river, people arrived at something very special close to its banks. It was a pool of water fed by a spring bubbling out of the ground from which steam rose due to the temperature of the water, a constant 10 - 15 degrees. The impact must have been magical, mystical. It was a supply of fresh water for people and animals when the river was frozen. It is now known as Blick Mead. The water has the additional phenomena of containing an algae, called Hildenbrandia rivularus, which flourished in the water due to a combination of the warmth and of dappled light which results in flint cortex turning from blood red in the water to magenta on contact with air. The awesome colour could only add a sense of enchantment to the atmosphere, to the power of the place. Perhaps there was a health benefit from it, as yet to be discovered.

The river provided them with water for drinking and food in the form of fish and waterfowl. At the side of the banks grew reeds, such as reed mace, (bullrushes), and wild grasses to weave into baskets used to gather food - fruits, berries, leaves, nuts, fungi and wild cereal grain as they came into season. There is evidence of people living there from 8,820 BC, making it the oldest settlement in the British Isles.

When they explored their landscape further, they would have climbed a sharp slope of land rising west of the river. Reaching the top, they would have looked down on, to their eyes, a very unusual landscape - devoid of extensive woodland. Instead they would have seen small clumps of trees on open downland scattered with sarsen boulders. One of these was particularly large and running down the hillside from it in the direction of the midsummer solstice sunrise were soil stripes - perhaps seen as darker stripes of grass fed by the rainwater that had collected in the deep grooves of the chalk soil beneath. The tree clumps were predominantly of mixed pine and hazel. The discovery of the tiny bones of the yellow necked mouse confirm tall trees grew in the area, that being their habitat. Hazel needs sunlight in order to grow, indicating there were glades amongst the trees, grazed by animals such as red deer and with wild boar and wolves living in the woodland. Out in the open, grazed aurochs - huge beasts that looked similar to bison. Herds of these huge animals would have devoured and demolished vast amounts of vegetation. Young trees would not have survived them so may have been the reason why there were so few trees in this particular area, giving it a similar appearance to the prairies of North America, which are grazed by herds of bison.

Mesolithic Post Holes

The first evidence people left of their awareness of this area is a post hole dating to 8,000 BC. Into a pit a metre in diameter, the massive trunk of a Scots Pine tree was placed. People would have had to travel twenty miles to the north or south to find such a tree as they do not grow on chalk downland. Five hundred years later, 7,500 BC, long after the first post had rotted away, a second was set up a short distance away. Lacking any real evidence for their purpose, it is generally considered that they may have been used as totem poles, using the North American Indians for analogy, linking earth and heaven. The posts could each have been aligned to important moon rises or sun rises or constellations.

The people who set the first post up were living 1,500 years after the end of the last Ice Age. They may have had an oral tradition that told of the extended periods of cold and dark experienced during that time, stories trying to make sense of the world around them. Throughout the Stone Ages people had lived close to nature and were aware of their dependency on her moods. They observed the stars and their courses. They may have considered that the effect of astronomical events were responsible for events on earth. Everything they saw and experienced had a spirit which could be personified in stories and myths. By 8,000 BC the climate was more settled and there was plenty to eat, which would have made life easier in contrast with the difficulty of struggling for survival in the harsh conditions of the Ice Age. They may have attributed the positions of the constellations as responsible for this change, of the cosmic harmony they now experienced. The first massive timber may therefore have been set up as, or representative of, the axis on which the Earth spins, an axis mundi - the imaginary pole that goes through Earth, around which it revolves, holding it in its position in the heavens, a structure to hold the world in balance. Of-course there can be no proof of this - unless one day science discovers that the cognitive responses leave indelible impressions on bone and we learn something of how our ancestors thought.

It was not necessarily representative of the axis of the physical world. There are worldwide legends of an axis mundi holding the world in place be it pillar or tree, which can also be the link between shamanic realms. As such it could link the tiered cosmos of the spirit realms - Upper, Middle and Lower worlds - once familiar to all but which through the ages became the province of the shaman. Shamanism includes the oldest rites, magic, rituals known to mankind. Shamans act as intermediaries between the spirit and the human worlds. They reach altered states of consciousness through rituals brought about through such activities as drumming, ingesting drugs, dance, fasting, pain in order to channel information from the spirit world to this world, such as where to hunt, or to appeal for propitious weather conditions. They learnt to 'get inside' the animal they were tracking, to take it on into their own being, to think what it had been thinking, feel what it had been feeling when it left its track in order to find it, becoming the animal. It had left something of its energy along with its track, which the shaman could feel. The wearing of masks made from skulls with antlers may have been a way of helping to achieve this or a form of camouflage - or both. Aspects of shamanism are depicted in Palaeolithic cave and rock art throughout the world. Worldwide imagery of creation mythology includes a world tree, as representative of an axis mundi, with roots in the underworld, trunk in the present world and branches in the heavens. The most well known is the Norse Yggdrasil. In other parts of the world, aurochs represented the present world and representations guarded the axis mundi and the route between the tiers of the cosmos - around the Mesolithic posts they roamed freely.

Whatever they were and however they were used, the presence of the posts indicates that this was an area that people returned to. The hunter-gatherer people living by the river were semi-nomadic - if they knew that salmon were leaping at a certain time of year in a particular place along a river, then they would have returned to it. The posts may each have been set up to mark the route the aurochs took through the landscape towards their water source. They may have provided long sighting lines to natural features in the landscape or to other posts as yet undiscovered and used to predict when this would happen by the position of sunrises and sunsets, the risings of the moon by night and movements of the constellations. Setting up the posts may have been instigated by the shaman, requiring effort from the people and 'magic' from him, to aid him to 'climb the tree' and 'take flight amongst the stars' as he observed the night sky, monitoring with posts alignments of the heavenly bodies, by which he could predict migratory movement of aurochs. After performing the magic of the hunt successfully, perhaps they then celebrated by dancing, feasting and storytelling around their 'totem pole.'

Around 6,250 BC, a third Scots pine post was set up. This date coincides with the date that the land bridge was disappearing between Britain and Europe. The coastline constantly changes. Between 60,000 - 6,250 BC, Britain gradually became cut off from mainland Europe, the final land bridge between the two disappearing in a single generation around 6,250 BC. Although not set up together, the post holes follow an almost west - east alignment which may reference the highest point east. (Now called Beacon Hill). People were living in and returning to the area from across the country. They also had a direct route along the river to the sea. Around 6,250 BC, water levels were increasing by 13 mm a year. The last generation of people to have walked between Europe and Britain would have been able to remember walking, then paddling, then wading before having to make the journey by boat. Perhaps it seemed that the world was flooding again, as it had done at the end of the last Ice Age and remembered in oral traditions. Setting up the third post may have been an attempt to fix the constellations in place so they could not cause the world to flood. However, within living memory the coastline changed and Britain became an island. Socially, the people were forming a group identity.

By the time that the third timber was set up, the area by the warm spring was an established settlement, rather than a hunting camp, or at least a base that groups returned to regularly. It is the discovery of over 200 pieces of aurochs bone which provides the evidence for this. Now extinct, an aurochs was twice the size of a cow. One has a radio carbon date of 6,250 BC and it has been suggested that it was a yearling and would have weighed about one and a half tons. The meat from an aurochs would have fed a gathering of 100 people - at a time when the total population in Britain and Ireland was 20,000 - 30,000. The aurochs had been cooked - dry heat cooking - and is the first evidence of cooked food in Britain and Ireland. Hunting, killing, preparing and cooking the animal was a huge communal undertaking. The hunting and feasting may have taken on a ritual quality, recognising that the animal gave his all for them - his body to feed them, his skin to clothe them, to shelter them, his bones for implements, his hooves for glue and for any other things. That he served by giving himself. Gathering together for a communal activity such as hunting and feasting gave a sense of oneness - the sharing of food from a single source, becoming one with it - absorbing its spirit - and with one another and may be been the embryonic beginnings of ritual and worship.

Circular impressions close to the spring can be seen on Google Earth, roughly the size of a dwelling. Although at this time they have not been fully investigated, there are high magnetic readings close to the circular marks indicating fire, suggesting that this was where people lived. Perhaps around these fires, people drew together and spoke of prolonged periods of darkness and cold during the Ice Age, of constellations whose movements controlled this, of stars that had led them over continents, of the flight of the shaman, of the warm spring, of their hunting exploits. They may have told stories to explain the seen and unseen forces in the world around them.

Flint tools have been found at Blick Mead dating from the same period of time. Within a trench 6m x 4m, at the spring, a 12 cm layer of pristine flint tools has been found, numbering over 32,000 at the time of writing. Exquisitely crafted, these flint tools fulfilled an extraordinary variety of uses. Tools for hunting - some of which have the aerodynamics of a stealth bomber, designed for maximum impact and cutting ability. There are 'engineering' tools to make other tools - such a cutting tool for arrow shafts. Tools for skinning an animal, for cutting the meat, for preparing the skin as clothing. Sometimes the cortex was deliberately left as a finger grip - and from this it can be seen that some of the people were right handed, some left handed. The nearest flint mine was a short distance away. However, some tools are of Brandon flint, from East Anglia, indicating that people were travelling from considerable distances. They returned to the spring with its warm water, where they deposited unused tools, suggesting they were placed as offerings. In turn, this implies that for them the spring was a specially cherished place, a place of enchantment.

Causewayed Enclosures

Over the ensuing 2,000 years the varieties of trees growing in the area increased. Oak, lime, pine, birch, elm, hawthorn and crab apple trees and hazel grew in clumps. The climate was much warmer than it is now. Forest and vegetation grew rapidly in what had become a sub tropical, warm, damp climate. There is some evidence that clearance activity of forest areas was done at this time. Ferns and brackens were growing and in the open amongst the grasses grew meadow flowers. The grassland continued to be grazed by deer and aurochs.

We have very little evidence to understand what might have been happening in this area between 6,250 and 4,000 BC. People continued to move seasonally and live in temporary settlements but by 4,000 BC were beginning to collect seed from wild cereal crops, plant it at a site convenient to themselves and settle nearby - although still on a semi-nomadic basis. On the open downland, scattered deposits of sarsen stone remained. The soil was rich and fertile, good for growing crops and providing rich pastureland for animals such as aurochs, deer and wild boar. The nearby river continued to give access to the coast and had probably become an early trading route. Over the marshes and river valleys hung mists and rainbows. It was a land where legend had life, born from tales told around night fires. They recognised that the Earth, the seasons and the weather were the great arbitrators of their lives. Perhaps people personified the invisible forces at work in the universe, giving them a human or animal form that captured the essence of that force and aligning themselves with it. A recognition of unseen energies may have given birth to superstition - that certain acts could appease these energies. They may have offered something of themselves, such as the tools they had deposited at Blick Mead, as an exchange of energy. This acknowledgement and respect may have led to reverence and eventually to worship.

It was not until 4,000 BC that people started to shape their landscape with monuments and when they did, one of the reasons appears to have been for ceremonial gathering. One such gathering area was the causewayed enclosure - areas of land, up to several hundred metres across, enclosed by ditches with internal banks. The solid land that bridges the ditch forms causeways, which distinguishes this type of structure. The spring at Blick Mead was an established gathering place and this may be the reason why man-made structures appear very much later in the area than in other places. One was built around 3,650 BC about three miles north of where the Mesolithic posts had stood, making it one of the last to be built in the country. (It is now called Robin Hood's Ball). Building was a communal activity, in the way they had, in the past, gathered together to hunt. This communal undertaking helped to form a social group. They built a place to return to that had not been shaped by unseen forces but with their own energy. They were places to gather, to share experience. Gathering together at such places may have been to meet, for celebration and to trade. At such times they exchanged not only goods and cattle but perhaps women too. The building of enclosures was not something that would have been undertaken if there was not enough food for their families as that would have been a far more important priority. Causewayed enclosures were being built by an assemblage of people, possibly lineage groups, who worked together. They may have felt ownership for the land they had enclosed, rather than territorial for areas of land. At another causewayed enclosure, Crickley Hill in Gloucestershire, there is the first archaeological evidence of a battle. It may have been an attempt to take over the resources of the people living there or perceived injustices may have built up over generations. Ownership, wealth and materialism seem to arrived with the earliest dabblings with agriculture.

Long Barrows

Another early man-made structure of a similar time was the long barrow. These may have developed in eastern Europe. In that area, houses - which were rectangular - appear to have been abandoned when the householder died, eventually decaying into a mound. This evolved to become specially built domains for the dead, mimicking the homes they had lived in.

By the time this practice reached Britain some, at least, were built as territorial markers on high ridges of land, reaching higher towards the heavens, looked up to and to be seen from a distance. Long barrows are best known for their use as mortuary chambers. Highly visible as they were, built in liminal places between earth and sky, they may have acted as a reminder of the closeness and the oneness with the ancestors. Sometimes they were built on top of middens, dumps for domestic rubbish. Long barrows did not appear in the Blick Mead landscape until 3,600 BC, which was again later than in the rest of it by four hundred years. Below them, people lived out their lives as nomadic pastoralists, supplementing their diet by hunting.

Long barrows are comprised of chambers constructed of stone or wood, according to the available materials in the locality. Sometimes they had porches. On the chalk downland of Salisbury Plain, they were built as ovals of wooden posts, which are likely to have had hurdle walls roofed over with turfs. One had a timber façade, arcing out from the main structure like horns. The visible timbers may have been decorated by painting or carving. Finally, soil was mounded over the structure, leaving the porch end open for access to the cave-like recesses inside. Around the structure was a bank and ditch, which may have formed not only a physical boundary but also a psychological one - this was a special place, set aside from everyday life. They were usually used as communal burial places, often returned to and used by many generations, between 4,000 - 3,000 BC. Grave goods were not a feature of long barrows but they did occasionally deposit cattle and aurochs bone and red deer antlers. One out of the fifteen in the immediate landscape was very unusual in that it contained the body of just one man, (his skeleton and a reconstruction of his head is now on display in the Stonehenge Visitors' Centre), suggesting he was very important, perhaps a particularly powerful shaman.

Bones in long barrows were usually disarticulated, implying that bodies under went sky burials - exposure on platforms for the elements to deal with prior to deposition. They are often found with arm bones in one chamber, leg bones in another and skulls, sometimes smashed, in another. Instead of discarding their dead, complex burial rituals were evolving. The dead - grandfathers, grandmothers, fathers, mothers - were revisited, indicating that there was some sort of continuing relationship with departed ancestors. When someone died, that person became an ancestor who could arbitrate in the spirit world on behalf of the living for beneficial conditions such as favourable weather, fertile crops, healthy livestock. Shamans could have acted as intermediaries. Part of the activities around a long barrow may have involved aiding the spirits to continue on their spiritual journey. Interaction with the dead may have been conducted by an individual such as a seer or shaman who not only looked after them but also invited them to look after the living, to mediate with the cosmos on their behalf. It may have been that it was the shaman, who continued to seek out food sources for the group, who had increasing influence and power, enabling him to organise groups of people to build and for rituals.

In many societies across the world shamans leave their bodies through trance in order to travel not only in search of a food source but also to travel through other parts of the cosmos in search of information to help their people, information for the benefit of the community as a whole and also for individuals. Information such as finding food and ensuring fertility of crops and animals. In a state of trance, they visit the upper, middle and lower realms. Sometimes visions are induced by hunger, dancing, drugs, extreme pain - or simply by drumming, which can align brain waves with the pulse of the earth. Visions can give a sense of passing through a tunnel towards light and of flight, both of which are generated by neurological mechanisms in the human nervous system, producing similar experience regardless of culture, language and time. The apparently external experience is internal, a feeling of flight within the brain as a response to external stimuli. Neurologically generated experiences are elements that appear across the world in prehistoric art and in mythology alongside global natural phenomena. Perhaps long barrows were designed in imitation of these neurological responses so people could experience for themselves the dark tunnels of vision leading to the light, which aided contact with the ancestors. The dark, man-made cave may have represented the Lowerworld, or Underworld, regions visited by the shaman, places of non-ordinary reality which provided answers to specific questions.

Long barrows may have had other uses in addition to deposition of bones. They may have been used for initiation and rites of passage between childhood and maturity. Imagine being taken into the dark underworld interior in the evening as the light fades, perhaps by the elders or the shaman, being left there maybe with a small fire flickering against the uneven walls and spending the night amongst the ancestors. We might see that now as an experience of untold terror brought forth from the imagination as one reached into the recesses of one's own soul to reach an insight and understanding of one's own deep self before being reborn from the earthen tomb at first light. They may have viewed it with anticipation, familiar with respect for the ancestors from earliest childhood, looking forward to communing with them for themselves, for deepening their perception of life.

Additionally, it would seem that at special times people came to them to gather, to share experience, to perform ceremonies, to tell stories - mythology which passed down the generations wisdom and arcane knowledge of the universe, including movements of the heavenly bodies that governed their existence. Some ceremonies may have been to encourage crops to grow. The officiator of these may himself have stood on the man-made hill, to see and be seen, raised socially by his esoteric knowledge. Perhaps it was also from this raised area it was perceived that the spirits of the ancestors flew home.

The ground immediately around a barrow tends to be

compacted, as though with much use, suggesting that dancing and feasting may have taken place as part of the ceremony. This was almost certainly a protracted affair and this prehistoric tradition is continued right up to our own time in events such as weddings, which are followed by a reception and funerals, which are followed by a wake. As other peoples infiltrated the landscape, perhaps the barrows entered into British folklore as the hollow hills of faery - hills that, traditionally, appeared and disappeared at will, places of feasting and dancing, not quite part of the ordinary world, places from whence it was difficult to return.

The Heel Stone

The open landscape west of the spring, in the centre of which the Mesolithic posts had stood, was open with well-established, (grazed), grassland scattered with sarsens and with some wooded areas. Periglacial stripes may also have been visible, perhaps as darker stripes of vegetation, some of which ran down the hillside in the direction of the midsummer solstice sunrise and up the hillside in the direction of the midwinter solstice sunset towards a huge recumbent sarsen stone. At some point this stone was hoisted upright, to stand in the socket of its own hole. It may have been raised as early as 6,000 - 4,000 BC. It is now called the Heel Stone. There are a number of different versions of how it got its name, which may hint at its significance. The Celts, (associated with the late Bronze Age and Iron Age), tended to describe features of the landscape rather than give them names. For example, 'Avon' is Celtic for river - there are five River Avons in England. They called the stone 'clach na freos heol,' (pronounced clack na friar's heel). The phrase means 'the stone of the rising sun'. People still watch for the Midsummer sun to rise over this stone. Other languages can also provide clues to the naming of the Heel Stone. In Egypt, 'hele' means the sun, (Heliopolis - the city of the sun). In Saxon, 'helan' means to hide. The sun, just after rising, appears to hide behind the Heel Stone before rising into full view.

Beyond the stone towards the direction of the midwinter sunset was a mound which may belong to this time, further referencing the midwinter solstice sun set or the midsummer solstice sun rise directly over the stone. There are pits on the near horizon north east and north west of the Heel Stone which may belong to the time when the stone was raised, marking the position the midsummer solstice rises as seen from the stone and another marking where it sets. The exact nature of the features of the pits has yet to be determined - but their existence is revealed as pits five metres across and one and a half metres deep.

The sun now rises slightly to the west of the Heel Stone and the socket of a companion stone has been discovered a short distance away. The pair were not a symmetrical pair and we have no date for the second stone. People may have stood where they could see the midwinter solstice sunsets to the south west and midsummer solstice sunrises to the north east between the two. The midwinter solstice marks an important turning point in the year darkness and death hold nature in thraldom; no life stirs in the ground. Then, after the shortest, darkest day of the dying year the old sun ceases to decline and, miraculously, a newborn sun rises and the days grow lighter and longer, the earth starts to spring back into its growing season again and nature reasserts its life-force.

Cursus

Approximately 3,600 - 3,300 BC, half a mile north of the Heel Stone, people built an earthwork monument consisting of parallel chalk banks that enclosed an elongated area 1.75 miles long, west to east towards the highest land on the far horizon. Its white chalk banks would have been very prominent, highly visible from a considerable distance. It is now known as the Cursus. At the eastern end, was a long barrow 60 metres long and 3 metres high which was constructed at approximately the same time, possibly earlier. The Cursus is the largest and most labour intensive earthwork monument in the vicinity - it has been estimated that 20,000 tons of chalk were excavated in order to create it.

The high ridge of land on which it was built forms a watershed and this natural division of land may have been an ancient route for animals - such as migrating aurochs - and people between the valleys either side from Mesolithic times. It could have been built as a closure, when an ancient route went out of use in favour of a new one.

The Cursus encloses the two pits marking the positions of the midsummer solstice sunrise and sunset. They may be Mesolithic or they may have been dug after the Cursus as we have no dates for them as yet. The sunrise pit was visible from the Heel Stone but the sunset pit was hidden by a ridge of land, suggesting that the only way its position could be determined was if smoke was rising from it. This gives rise to the suggestion that they may have been used as fire pits, lit to show where the sun would set and rise.

The length between theses pits is the shortest distance the sun is 'underground' at night. There may have been night long or day long rituals at the solstice. According to the testimony of old religions, such as those of Ancient Egypt, the Sun was born from an ark each morning. The spirit of the dying sun was caught in the ark at sunset, which was then carried throughout the night to be reborn from it in the new days' sunrise. Could the Cursus have been such an ark? In Egypt the sun's appearance during the day and disappearance at night was seen as being the inspiration and expiration of God. In the days before people communicated with writing, the ark was an important symbol through many different creeds. It always seems to have duality of purpose - to give birth and to carry the souls of the dead away. The Cursus may have formed a link between the ancestors and the sun, especially stretching as it does from a long barrow at its eastern end. It may therefore have had a ceremonial and ritual function, including those surrounding the burial of the dead.

PART TWO

Building the Monument

The Henge c.3,000 BC

By 3,000 BC, the area around the Heel Stone remained widespread grassland in an open landscape, with some wooded areas. To the north, vegetation had grown on the banks of the Cursus so it was a less obvious feature. To the east was a high ridge of land above the banks of the river beside which was a warm spring, which people had been returning to for 5,000 years.

People had lived in this country as hunter-gatherers with a knowledge of astronomy. Perhaps early observation of the night sky developed from genetic memory before the time when men stood upright, becoming *homo erectus*, when in order to arrive somewhere propitious for survival we navigated our Earth by sensing its energy lines, a hint of memory of covering vast distances. When we looked up and saw the shapes in the night sky walking with us, instinctively following them as they guided us through our world. From this ancestral memory of our earliest instincts, the seeds of astronomy were sown. It is something still remembered in stories told amongst the Australian aborigines from 40,000 years ago.

Early experiments with agriculture had not been successful and may have failed due to pests or to a climate crisis resulting in arable failure. Now people were planting seed they had gathered, at a site convenient to themselves, where they wanted it to grow, using their knowledge of astronomy to sow and reap at the most propitious times. We do not know what prompted them to mimic nature by attempting to master it. Previously they had hunted wild animals but now they were starting to domesticate them. Farming is more labour intensive than hunter gathering - both plants and animals are more prone to disease. Animals have to be fed and protected. Perhaps it was at this time people were developing a sense of ego, of separate identity rather than wholeness within a group and felt it was necessary to have 'control' over nature. Control came in exchange for responsibility - if they did not look after the animals and plants, they would not thrive. Perhaps as a result, interceding with the unseen forces which affected their labours began to take a more structured ritual form. The advent of agriculture may have heralded religion, where some people gained mastery not only over the land and the livestock but also over other people and their belief systems. Hunter-gatherer groups may have relied on the services of their shaman to lead them to finding food. Some shamans had animal spirit helpers to aid them amongst herds of wild animals. By possessing an animal physically, this service would become less important so that their attitude to ritual would change direction. Shamans had other skills, such as healing and as ritual specialists and it may have been at this time that they became a priestly caste. Groups continued to gather together seasonally. They had learnt to shape the landscape by building together. These were the people responsible for building the first phases of the monument we now call Stonehenge - farmers and astronomers with a high technical ability.

It was c.3,050 - 3,000 BC that people started to build in an area that had already been considered special for millennia by the inhabitants of Salisbury Plain. They dug a circular ditch and used the excavated chalk soil to build a two metre high circular bank, 100 metres in diameter. They used antlers as picks and ox shoulder blades as shovels. The accuracy of the circle was likely to have been formed by placing a peg in the centre and attaching one end of a rope to it and the other to a person. By then walking at the full stretch of the rope, a perfect circle is formed. Another method to form a circle is by using up to sixteen lengths of rope radiating outwards. One of the strongest plant fibres used at this time to make rope was made from the fibre of nettles bound together.

Cremated human bone was placed in the ditch and animal bones, skulls and flints were placed, ritualistically. Some of them were of considerable age, notably ox jaw bones which were three hundred years older than the ditch itself. It is quite likely that they had been kept as trophies, stories of their acquisition woven into the fabric of the developing society. Some of the positions seem to indicate significant moon risings. There may also have been a symbolic quartering of the site based on solar rising and setting points.

Cut from the hillside in gleaming white chalk, the circular bank would have stood out as a landmark on the landscape in the way the Cursus had done half a millennium previously. It was dug on the shoulder of a shallow slope that gradually steepened downwards in the east into a coomb. (Now known as Stonehenge Bottom). It would not have been possible to see in from the outside or out from inside, demarcating it from everyday life. As with the causewayed enclosures, there are bridges of land across the ditch which may not only have allowed different directional entrance but may have allowed the effects of whatever was happening in the centre to flow out across the land. It had a main access gap facing towards the north east. It may have provided a false horizon from where they could observe the movements of the sun, moon stars, planets, constellations. Certainly just at the main entrance there have been discovered six years' worth of observational post holes, pits which contained timber posts. This was a period of time when the most northerly risings of the moon were observed and the positions plotted with wooden posts set in the hillside. However, the period of six years was not six solar years but six lunar years. A lunar year is the length of time that passes between the moon rising in the exact same position on the horizon with the exact same pattern of constellations behind it. We now call this the Metonic cycle, after the Greek astronomer Meton who wrote of the phenomena in the C5th BC, two and a half thousand years after this was plotted at the henge entrance. As this is 18.61 of our Earth years, that means the risings of the moon were watched and plotted over a total period of 111 years - six lunar years - until a pattern began to form as to where they could expect the moon to rise. Every third lunar year, the moon also rises in the same phase - so, for example, if it rises as a full moon, it will be fifty six years before it rises again as a full moon in the same position on the horizon with the same pattern of constellations behind. They would have seen this during the period of observation plotted with the posts. Several generations of people would have lived during this time so there must have been a significant reason for such prolonged observation to continue. Rituals may have developed around these observations, leading to a modern interpretation that they indicate the practise of moon worship. There are post holes in the centre of the henge indicating that the most southerly risings were also observed.

As well as a place to observe the heavens, it may have been used for gatherings, times when communal decisions were made. A place to bring joys, angers, ills, celebrations, grievances to heal, to meet in a circle and feel the wholeness. Where all were equally important and responsible. It was probably also used for ceremonies. Ancient understanding, wisdom and experience of nature responding to the sun, moon, planets and constellations led to people aligning themselves with the natural forces, impelling and imploring things outside of their control, probably initially through their shaman, or ritual specialist, using imitation magic.

Station Stones

At the time of writing, it has not been established whether the Station Stones were erected before or after the circular bank. Just inside it were four small stones geometrically opposed. The northerly and southerly ones stood in two small ring ditches, (small henges). The banks of the circular bank overlay them, so they would seem to be earlier features. There is a mound immediately south of where the stones stand, whose date and purpose is unknown. It is currently envisaged that a standing stone may once have stood on it, before the henge was built, contemporary with the Heel Stone and the two small ring ditches. It may have been a barrow. It may have been debris from a later dig.

It is likely that these boulders and others formerly lay nearby on the surface and were simply erected in convenient locations. Placing ropes diagonally between them, the crossing point gives the centre of the circle, so they may have been set up an engineering devise for the later structure.

Traditionally it has been thought that the Station Stones were erected in order to align significant sunrises which were important to the prehistoric farming community - risings which perhaps told them when to sow and reap their crops and indicated other important events in their farming calendar. Deliberately setting the positions of their devise would indicate duality of purpose with just this very simple structure.

Aubrey Holes

Within eight decades of the bank and ditch being built, people dug out a circle of fifty-six pits at equal distances all around the inside of the circular bank. The pits are now known as Aubrey holes. We do not know for certain what the what the purpose of these pits was. When they were first dug they may have been used initially as votive pits in which to make propitiatory and prophylactic libations to the spirits and forces that inhabited the Lowerworld and nether regions. They also placed cremations in the pits. The earliest of these dates back to 3,300 BC - people living 300 years before the pits were dug. People had brought their honoured dead to the site, suggesting they had an ongoing relationship with the ancestors and perhaps brought them to the area to sanctify the new site, so that their ancestors continued to watch over and care for them.

Fifty six is the number of years in three lunar years - when the moon rises in the same phase, the same position and with the same pattern of constellations behind - and also the number of days it takes for the moon to orbit the Earth twice. They could have had been used as a lunar calendar - predicting important gathering times/festivals based on it. They could also be used to predict eclipses of the sun. This may well have been a very important omen in prehistoric times, because it would have looked as though the moon was actually 'killing' or 'eating' the sun. People were very aware of the natural world around them and if they observed such occurrences as natural disasters which seemed to occur as a direct result of eclipses, they may have felt they needed to be forewarned of such events.

It is probable that there were other 'heavenly bodies' besides the moon and the sun which were important enough to the Neolithic people that they needed to track them, such as the rising of particular constellations. We know that the rising of the Pleiades over Egypt at a similar date in the springtime heralded the flooding of the Nile. When the waters subsided, the Egyptians planted their crops in the fertile silt thrown up from the river bed.

Obviously this flooding was of paramount importance to people whose livelihood was dependant on the land. If there was no harvest, the people did not eat - they starved. Thus fertility and growth of the land was linked very closely to survival and prosperity. In ancient times, according to legend, the king or leader was held responsible for this - if he did not provide seasons conducive to a good harvest, he was killed and replaced. He and the land were one. If he was good, the land was good. If he was fertile, the land was fertile. But if the land failed, then he had failed too. In Britain, Celtic folklore tells many tales of this. As the land in this country was much wetter than it is now - and certainly the River Avon was deeper and wider than now - perhaps in this country also the farmers waited for flood water to recede in the spring before planting their crops. In Egypt it was thought that the Nile could not flood unless the constellations were properly positioned - hence they went to great lengths to ensure that this happened. Similar efforts may have been made in this area.

As recently as the last millennium, medicine wheels have been set up in North America by the North American Plain Indians, representative of a Wheel of Life on Earth. They align with other stones or geographic features to indicate solstices and other planetary and astrological events, thereby monitoring similar events.

Bluestones
c.2,920 - 2,550 BC

By this time, approximately 5,000 years ago, people had developed from lineage groups to small communities to a society that had developed sufficiently and was sophisticated enough to organise a labour force. Up until this point in time, people had shaped their landscape by digging earthworks and raising large stones from recumbent to upright. People may been travelling from or to the Preseli mountains in Wales along an established route to the area on Salisbury Plain, where people had been returning and gathering for at least 6,000 years.

The mountains were a barrier, a last stronghold, between Britain and the chaotic waters that separated her from Ireland. Once Ireland had joined Wales but sea had flooded the lowlands between the two. Now it was necessary to make this journey by boat - highly dangerous, mentally and physically challenging. The mountain valleys may have been considered the entrance to the lower realms, the Lowerworld. Additionally, they may have seen the mountain tops as special, inhabited by unseen forces, linking the panoply of sky above to Earth. At 1,760 feet above sea level, Preseli Top dominates the landscape for miles around. The stone of the rocky outcrops is dark blue, like the blue of a summers' night and spangled with white flecks - like the silvery images of stars. It may have appeared that where the night sky touched Earth, it had left its image on the rocks, the 'bones' of the Earth. The night, with its important constellations and its waxing and waning moon, still important for its 'control' over or 'effect' on the land. The people had a reverence for the sky. It may have seemed that the rock was a talisman for controlling the night. This idea was not necessarily new to them - bluestone has been found in long barrows in the area, built a thousand years before the henge, so they may have been following a long tradition of bringing this special stone to the area. Either way they may have seen themselves as retrieving the stone from another realm, another reality and transporting it to an area that was special to them an area to where people had been returning and gathering for 5,000 years.

Furthermore, the people who lived in the Welsh mountains may have noticed that the unseen spirits of the stones added healing properties to the spring water the gushed from and rushed over the rock and that by bathing in the water, they might be cured of almost any ailment. The water in the spring at Blick Mead may have had reputed healing properties. They could not take the water to the mountains but something of the mountains could be brought to the spring.

Around ten percent of bluestones have a curious musical property. When struck by a hammer stone, they ring like a bell or resound like a gong rather than making the usual stone against stone sound. It may have seemed that the stones were talking, that they could be used as oracles. Especially if people, particularly the shamans, participated in ritually using the psilocybin mushrooms that grew in the area. Even without the use of mushrooms, ritually produced sounds such as drumming can reputedly make enormous stones to appear to shimmy as though dancing.

So it was that soon after 3,000 BC bluestone, spotted dolerite, was taken from the Preseli mountains - a mythic otherworldly place - and brought to Salisbury Plain, a special place of gathering for 5,000 years. It was a distance of 150 miles. Each stone weighs 2 - 4 tons. Some of them may have already been standing in a configuration in the Preseli mountains. The initial part of the journey was overland, perhaps taking them on dry sledges, perhaps mounting them on wooden rollers. Use of wooden rollers would have reduced the number of people needed to move each one by almost a third but it would certainly have taken two to three dozen men to move each one. One group would need to pull on ropes attached to the stone and another group to constantly bring the timber rollers that came from the back of the stone to the front. This alone would have meant being sufficiently organised to work in unison. The stone movers probably began by setting up a rhythm, by singing, so that they could all work together. Once movement of the stone began, it would have moved across the landscape more readily, to the music of the singing, as if by magic. Thus the notion of moving heavy stone by music and magic may have entered into their folklore.

There are several suggested routes. All of them include crossing water. Travel by water is very efficient in terms of effort and labour to move heavy goods. A route overland would have been exceptionally difficult, even if the stones had been passed from community to community. The first few miles of the journey would necessarily have been overland. It has been suggested that they took to the sea at Milford Haven, possibly using rafts which were best able to withstand sea. They would have been large enough to carry not only a stone but also the people needed to manoeuvre it. They would have needed to keep sufficiently far from the shore to avoid rough waves, submerged rocks and swirling currents. Once they had navigated the estuary of the Severn, they could have continued by sea around the coast but probably not too close to it, where the sea is rougher. This means that if a raft sank taking its bluestone with it, it would be too deep under the sea for us to find it as evidence of the route taken. They continued to the mouth of the River Avon and from there towards Blick Mead. On entering the river, the rafts would have been too large to steer along the river. Boats such as three dugout canoes lashed together, with a stone strapped across it transversely would have accomplished it. A considerably shorter route would have been to utilise the rivers of Southern England from the Severn, going along the Bristol Avon, joining the River Frome above Bath, unloading them and transporting them at the shortest point between the Frome and the River Wylye - a distance overland of about six miles. There is no real evidence but this may have been a route known to the stone movers. When Boles Barrow, a long barrow three miles north of the Wylye, at Heytesbury, (approximately twelve miles west of Blick Mead), was excavated in the C19[th] it was found to contain a bluestone. They could have continued along the Wylye to where it meets the River Avon and along it, again towards their final destination.

The stones were unloaded on the banks of the river approximately half a mile south of Blick Mead. Glaciation during the Ice Age had caused flints to roll down the hillside to the river bank, providing a hard and durable surface. The slope of the bank was further reinforced by 'plastering' it with silt and flints, creating an area of compacted chalk with cut, evenly sized flints driven in to the surface thereby copying the one created naturally by glaciation. The disembarkation point was possibly marked by a ring ditch. Too small for a barrow, its dimensions match those of the ring ditch around the Heel Stone. In the centre stood a sarsen stone, probably one local to the landscape. A 10 metre circle of 27 bluestones stood on the banks dating to between 3,000 and 2,400 BC. (Now known as Bluestonehenge or West Amesbury henge). The circle may have been built as a marker for the bluestones destination, a ceremonial site to celebrate that part of the journey - at this time we cannot be sure. Although collectively termed as bluestones, not all are spotted dolerites from the Preseli mountains. There are also unspotted dolerites, rhyolites and tuffs. Stones were brought from a variety of sources, perhaps by different communities contributing to a communal project.

From the river, they were dragged the rest of the way to the site, again perhaps using sledges and rollers. They went along the least steep route, ascending from the river, going along the high ridge of land, descending into a shallow coomb before ascending the final slope in the direction of the midwinter solstice sunset. The distance from the river to the henge is two miles. Henges were often linked to running water, although this is the longest known link. In this way the total distance travelled overland would have been just twenty four miles, leaving the majority of the way to be traversed by water.

Having brought them to the site, they erected the bluestones in the Aubrey Holes, approximately 2,900 B.C. This date means that it was a very early stone circle. They had - perhaps - brought the spirits of the mountain tops to dwell with the spirits of the Lowerworld. Some of the holes may have held timber posts, rather than stone. Whichever fabric was used as markers, cremation burials continued to be placed close to the Aubrey Holes. In placing the ancestors close to the ringing bluestones, they may have been perpetuating a tradition of communicating with their ancestors, of talking to them, of the ancestors speaking to them through the stones.

The stones could have been set up as an embodiment of the heavens, whose movements they were familiar with, built after the pattern of the world. It may have been used subsequently as an astronomical observatory. It may have been used as a lunar calendar. It may have been used for gatherings and markets, in much the same was as causewayed enclosures were used. It may have been used as a court where justice was dispensed in the presence of their ancestors. By this time it is likely that rituals had developed in which case they would probably have been its most important function. Rituals may have evolved from the prolonged observation - indicated by the timber post holes at the access gap - and respect of the celestial bodies. They may have been beseeching the unseen forces that controlled their world that they spoke of in their stories. Deposition of the ancestors suggests that rituals had continued to evolve in regard to the dead, as indicated by the age of the cremations when deposited. The circular bank and its bluestones would have had more than one use - the measure of any good tool is simplicity of design and multiplicity of purpose. The site was used almost continually over the next few centuries.

Sarsen Phase
2,660 BC onwards

There were many settlements along the River Avon, which was still providing a trading route along its course and out to the coast, as well as water for everyday use. Blick Mead continued to be inhabited. The banks of the Cursus were silting up so it was a less obvious feature of the landscape. Long barrows had been out of use as mortuary chambers for half a millennium but their power would have been remembered in oral traditions and people are likely to have continued to visit them. The ritual focus had become the nearby circular henge bank - silting up and grassed over - with its bluestones, Heel Stone and Station Stones. Although we tend to think that the next phase of building was the idea of one mind, conceptualised as a whole before bringing the raw materials, the design may have evolved gradually as the builders developed their skills.

During the centuries since the henge had been built, a great many changes and developments had been taking place. People were starting to establish more permanent settlements as early pastoralists and agriculturalists. They grew cereal crops. They kept cattle such as a domesticated variety of cows introduced from Europe, sheep or goats and pigs. Across the other side of the world, a few centuries later, the biblical Abraham made his epic journey around the fertile crescent as a nomadic pastoralist, circa 1,900 BC. They traded in goods and commodities. They still retained an awareness of their dependence on the Earth, the weather, the seasons and especially the sun, so by this time they had become increasingly focused on the sun.

Twenty miles north of the henge - a day's walk away - are the Marlborough Downs. Millions of years previously the range of these hills formed the cliffs of the southern coast of England. Over time the sandy cliffs fossilised to become sandstone. This sounds as though it would be a soft stone but because it is fused together with quartz, it is a particularly hard type of stone. We call it sarsen. The stone lies on the surface of the earth as huge monoliths so they do not have to be quarried, just carefully selected for size and shape. They occur within a very small area. People living close to the source had learnt how to move them and erect them. They had used six hundred stones to form the two great stone circles of Avebury with two avenues coiling out of them. It must have attracted huge numbers of people for important gatherings. Although the activities there probably had a different focus perhaps it threatened to eclipse the gatherings at the bluestone circle. Perhaps they noticed special properties in the sarsens. Perhaps it was the people of Avebury that brought their stones to the bluestone circle, adding their energy to it.

This was the source from where sarsen stones were selected in order to take to the henge near Blick Mead. It was the nearest known supply of stone, stone which people had already learnt how to move.

We do not know why they were taken to their new destination. Maybe they were brought to unite groups of people, in the way that the bluestones may have been. However, if it was simply that two groups of people were amalgamating, it would have been easier to take the bluestones to Avebury than to take the massive sarsens to them, suggesting that the gatherings at the bluestones remained the more important focus. Maybe it was believed that the quartz in the sarsens enhanced the healing properties of the bluestones.

Whatever the reason, it is believed that like the bluestones, the sarsens were transported the twenty mile distance from the Marlborough Downs by taking them overland on wooden rollers or sledges. We know they can be moved in this way but we cannot be certain this was how it was done. Bringing the sarsens was a much larger operation than transporting the bluestones, as the sarsen stones weigh between fifteen and fifty tons each. This indicates that four and a half thousand years ago, people had a society sufficiently developed to organise the huge number of people needed for such a project, which quite an achievement. It would have taken several hundred men seven weeks in man hours to bring the largest of the stones to their new destination. As eighty were brought, that would have been a whole decade in man hours. Of-course, we have no idea of what labour force was available to them or how long it actually took to bring all the stones to the site but it may well have taken longer than a single generation of stone movers. It would not have been possible to haul them in rainy seasons when the ground was waterlogged, for example, so the weather would have determined to some degree how quickly the work could be done. The huge labour force would have made it the most densely populated part of the country. Workers may have been attracted to the area by the promise of security, subsequently trading their labour for food, clothes and shelter not only for themselves but also their families. In fact the older and younger members of the community and the women may have provided these while the fittest men built, so it was very much a communal effort. As well as building the monument, they were also building the beginnings of a modern society. It must also have been a time of peace because it wouldn't be possible to build during a time of war. So into this settled period it would seem a feasible to suggest that a leader had grown to prominence who wanted to improve on the earlier building and all other known monuments, a leader who wanted a monument to reflect how rich and powerful he was. Whatever the original concept, it was probably understood than it would take more than a generation to complete.

The most likely route the stones were brought was down the steep escarpment of the Marlborough Downs over cereal grasses, across the highest and therefore least marshy land of the Vale of Pewsey, passing or more probably assembling at another major henge at Marden. It encloses 14 hectares, making it the largest henge in the country and is built near the source of the River Avon. From there, the stones were hauled up the equally steep escarpment of Salisbury Plain and then across the higher and flatter downland. Trees grew in sparse groups and may have provided timber for new rollers for the stones as they split. In places, cereals were grown but the downland was predominantly pastureland. The final part of the journey involved being hauled up towards the henge, perhaps following the line of the periglacial soil stripes towards the Heel Stone and the henge bank.

There are two other locations that a few of the sarsens may have originated from. Some may have been in the immediate vicinity. Periglacial processes around the area may have revealed sarsens that needed to be hauled only a short distance into the required positions. There are large depressions in the surrounding landscape to corroborate this. Weathered sarsen lying on the surface develops a crust which becomes very hard and resistant to shaping, so partially buried sarsen would be easier to shape and carve - highly advantageous.

It is possible that the occasional sarsen monolith was found south, in areas we now call Hampshire and Dorset. There may have been an arrangement whereby people from these regions made a contribution and an investment in the site by bringing a large, local stone.

The building material was ready and work was about to begin but the people involved in the project needed somewhere to live.

Durrington Walls
2,660 - 2,600 BC

Approximately one mile north of Blick Mead close to the river, the land curves into a fold forming a huge hollow. There may have been a spring to the north west of the curve. In the early part of the fourth millennium BC, this area had been cleared of trees. This is different to similar sites, which were built on open grassland. Possibly around this time, two trees at least had blown over and potsherds, dating roughly 3,800 BC, have been found in and around the throw hole. Meadow flowers such as bedstraw, bellflowers, bird's foot trefoil, buttercups, clovers, daisies, devil's bit scabious, red campion, rockrose and salad burnet grew amongst the grasses. Down by the river were sedges, marsh-marigold and burreed. The appearance of weeds such as black bindweed, docks, cleavers, (goosegrass), lesser stitchwort, fat hen, goosefoots, vetches/tares and knot grass indicate intensive land clearance as they do not grow amongst long grass. Flints had washed down the valley to the river creating a natural platform on the bank.

It was here that over fifty structures, dwellings and ceremonial buildings, were built. They were linked to the river by an Avenue. They were built 2,660 - 2,600 BC, the same time that the sarsens were being raised a mile and a quarter to the west.

The huts were approximately 5 m x 5 m, some sunken, walls built of woven strips of wood, (wattle). It would have taken an acre of coppiced hazel to produced sufficient wood for each house. They were plastered with cob - a mixture of chalk, straw and water. Floors were puddled chalk. They probably had tall, conical roofs, thatched with reeds and straw from alongside the river. Each house would have needed three acres of straw for its roof. Holes cut in the chalk close to the walls indicate that timbers were placed to support furniture such as beds and cupboards, similar in design to the stone houses at the other end of the country in Skara Brae, Scotland. Fires for heating and cooking burnt in the centre of the floor space with the smoke defusing through the thatch and out of the door. Houses may have developed from the building of long barrows, from ritual to domestic. This is a style of house found all over the country. It is thought that the initial purpose of the dwellings was for the large quantity of workers needed to erect the sarsen stones.

   Leading from the houses to the river was an Avenue, built over a naturally occurring platform of flints, washed down the slope at the end of the last Ice Age. People added a second layer of flints to this, compacting them into the chalk soil. It led from the dwellings in the direction of the midwinter sunrise. It is bordered by banks, making it 30 metres wide and 170 metres long. The flat part it is 15 metres wide.

   At the head of it, a ceremonial timber circle was erected, 40 metres in diameter, consisting of 6 concentric rings of posts. It was constructed in four phases during a period of less than a century. Named the Southern Circle, it is aligned to the Midsummer sunset and Midwinter sunrise. There was a second, smaller timber circle to the north of it. Beyond it further north were a group of flint mines. The timbers for the circles were brought at least ten miles from north or south.

Preparing the Sarsens

Just outside of the north east entrance into the henge, the journey to bring the sarsens to the henge was completed. Here the stones were shaped and dressed, ready to be raised. Sarsen is very difficult to work - it only splits horizontally and vertically and has a particularly high resistance to abrasion. On a scale of 1 to 10, diamonds are 10, steel is 6.7 and sarsen is 7, so it is harder to work than steel. Smoothing away dust particles was all they could do. The only tools they had to work against the stones were balls of the sarsen stone itself, called mauls, that they hammered away at the stone to shape it and dress it. It takes about an hour to remove six cubic inches of dust using this method and it has been estimated that over three million cubic inches were removed from the stones. The stones were shaped into blocks that tapered towards the end that would stand highest. The upper surface was smoothed away to leave a tenon joint ready to hold a lintel in place on top of them. The stones that were to be used as lintels were shaped to curve on both the inner and the outer sides so that when they were in position, they would form a perfect circle both on the inside and the outside. The under surface had mortise joints corresponding to the tenons of the upright to hold them neatly in place on top of them. Beneath the outer cortex of the stone that was shaped away, the stones were revealed as light, quite bright, grey in colour.

In addition to the mortise and tenon joints, tongue and groove joints were carved at the ends of the lintels of the outer circle. The tongue joint is a vertical protuberance at the end of the stone. The next stone had a vertical groove carved in it to fit the two firmly together. Unlike at other locations, this was not a simple stone circle but a building that mimicked the ceremonial timber structures at Durrington Walls. Joints that had been developed through working in wood were used in stone.

The circular bank at the access gap was shortened on one side and lengthened on the other so that the entrance to the site was now towards the direction of the Midsummer sunrise, indicating a shift in the orientation of their focus from moon to sun, on which, especially as agriculturalists, people recognised their dependence. This means that the subsequent stone circles had a slightly different centre to those of the henge bank and ditch and Aubrey Holes. Approaching it from the valley, up the slope towards the Heel Stone, is the direction of the midwinter solstice sunset, the most important orientation of the site. After the shortest day, the days grow longer and lighter and the earth springs back into its growing season again, which would have been very important to Neolithic farmers.

In the centre of the henge, the people started to raise the sarsen stones, creating the enigmatic and iconic image that we know of as Stonehenge today.

Sarsen Trilithons

We tend to think that there was an initial plan for the design of the monument. However, it evolved from the monuments already standing in the immediate vicinity of the henge - the Heel Stone, the Station Stones and the bluestones - and the ones that stood further from it, the Cursus and the long barrows. The Heel Stone and Station Stones provided solar and lunar alignments. Half a millennium previously, long barrows had gone out of use. Their structure mimicked the darkness of a natural cave and as well as their use as communal burial chambers, it can be surmised that other rituals and initiations took place within their recesses. There are structures called coves in other places, usually three sided, such as the cove at Avebury which are thought to imitate long barrows. Similarly, the horseshoe of trilithons may have been built as a descendant of the long barrow. The largest trilithon on its own would serve a similar function to a cove, enhancing the solstitial alignments with the Heel Stone. Perhaps this was the initial concept and the flanking trilithons that formed the horseshoe added shortly after, as people realised there was no limit to their building capabilities. The trilithon horseshoe alone would have been a place where rituals and initiations continued but instead of a man made earth mound separating the ritual specialists and initiates from the cosmos as with the long barrows, now the open structure allowed them integration with it. Instead of limited alignments, such as a doorway facing an equinox or solstice sunrise or specific moonrises, now multiple alignments could be viewed throughout the year. As well as communing with their ancestors, the builders may have been aware they were the ancestors of the future, that their wisdom would be passed through their children's children's children. They set their wisdom in stone and it reaches us still, even though we have yet to understand it fully.

The sarsens were erected as a horseshoe shape of five trilithons - two upright stones capped by a lintel stone across them. They ascend in size, the first and fifth originally being twenty feet high including their lintels, the second and fourth twenty one and a half feet high and the largest and central one was twenty four feet high. The horseshoe opened out towards the direction of the Midsummer sunrise. From the Heelstone, the midwinter solstice sun set through the largest trilithon. The partner and lintel of this one has now fallen but the remaining upright dominates the monument as the tallest stone on the site. It is the largest worked monolith in Britain and weighs close to fifty tons - heavier than a fully loaded articulated lorry or the weight of seven elephants. It has an overall length of 29' 8", eight feet of which are below the ground as its foundation. Its partner is only 24' tall overall, so less than four feet was below ground as foundation.

Raising the Sarsen Stones

In order to erect the uprights, the first thing it was necessary to do was to dig foundation pits in the chalk, using red deer antlers as a tool. These were used as picks to loosen the soil and then ox shoulder blades used as shovels to remove the soil. The uprights of the outer circle had foundations four or five feet deep, roughly a third of their own length. Little pieces of the antler chipped off into the pits and provide the material for radiocarbon dating this stage of building at Stonehenge, giving a date of 2,660 - 2,600 BC.

The ends of the sarsen stones were placed over the ends of the foundation pits, dropped down into them, possibly using weights to achieve this. They were then levered upright, the foundation pits having been reinforced with timbers to add resistance against the stone. They used ropes from hide, sinew or fibre, obtained from plants such as nettles. Another strong fibre from plant indigenous to this country is made from the bark of small leafed lime trees. The bark is put into mud for six weeks, during which time micro-organisms in the water eat away the resinous part of the bark. This leaves ten to twelve layers of very strong fibre. It is very likely that this method was known to the builders of Stonehenge.

The uprights were packed loosely with earth and some of the sarsen mauls that had been used to shape the stones. The latter may have been done ceremonially, returning all that had been taken from the Earth.

Erecting the uprights was only half the job, because then they had to get the lintels on the top. It is because the lintels are on the top that Stonehenge is classed as a building, rather than a stone circle. There are plenty of other stone circles, but as a building, Stonehenge is unique. What motivated them to create something so unique? What could they do here that could not be done in a stone circle? What happened here? These questions allow space for personal reflection and opinion.

The most likely method they would have used to raise the

lintels onto the uprights was with a series of wooden platforms. As there were plenty of trees growing in the area, there were plenty of materials to build in this way - also wood leaves no trace for the archaeologists to find. They could achieved the same with earthwork ramparts but there is no evidence of that amount of soil having been moved at Stonehenge.

Using a series of wooden platforms, they could have levered up first one end of a stone and put a platform under it, then levered up the other end and put another platform under, putting under more and more ramps until the lintel was higher than the tops of the uprights. It could then have been levered across and dropped down onto the tenon joints. The stones must have been lined up when they were carved to make sure the joints were in the right place. It would have been no good getting the lintels all the way to the top of the uprights and then discovering the joints were in the wrong place. Once in place, the upper surface formed a perfectly level surface, despite being built on a slope. It would have been necessary to bury the stones at different depths to achieve this.

A discrepancy is that the fallen lintel stone of the biggest trilithon, the Great Trilithon, not only has mortises to hold it onto its uprights, but there are what appear to be mortises on the upper surface too. As the most important trilithon, it seems highly unlikely that they made a mistake and simple turned the stone over, rather that the bowl shapes were there for a reason and could have been used for ritual purposes, such as holding fires to frame the setting midwinter sun. Recent surveying shows it is not the only lintel to have bowl shapes carved in its upper surface.

It is not known whether there was any significance in the number five to the ancient people. Knowledge of the cosmos was such an integral part of their lives, the trilithons could each represent one of the five planets visible from Earth with the naked eye. Nor is it known what was the significance of the horseshoe shape. It could have been a rough representation of the crescent moon worshipped there but if so, with all their skill they would surely have turned in the ends to form a proper crescent - besides, it would seem that the orientation of their worship had changed by this time.

The sarsen trilithons could represent a bull's horns, considered a very powerful symbol of rebirth and fertility at least since Mesolithic times - when the auroch gave his life for the survival of the people. It is highly likely that the monument was used at one time as a fertility temple, which is reasonable considering how aware people were of their dependency on fertility for survival - of their crops, their animals and themselves. Bull's horns were also the symbol of the Age of Taurus, the Bull and would be an appropriate design of this time. The bull symbol is frequently reflected in Egyptian art of this period as Apis and Mnevis, bull and cow deities. The setting midwinter solstice sun would thus be seen to set between the bull's horns.

By extending one's fingers around the periphery of vision in an open space, the framework of what we see is horseshoe shaped. Turning on the spot through 360 degrees the horizon is a circle. Standing at the centre of the open end of the horseshoe of trilithons, they frame the periphery of vision. The design could be a model of the world both as we see it and as we know it to be. Around it the sun, moon, planets and constellations turn on their eternal course.

It seems more likely that the sarsen trilithons were raised before the sarsen circle, although this is not necessarily so. Not only would the larger stones just not fit between the smaller gaps of the outer circle after it had been erected but more compellingly, excavations have shown they were pulled up from the outside and there would not be space to raise them with the outer circle already in place. The radiocarbon dating is inconclusive as there are so few artefacts to test in this way. The stones around the horseshoe may never have stood as a completed circle, which would leave space for the stones to be brought in - but not erected. There is enough space for four uprights - which would complete the circle - whose existence has never been certain. Parch marks in prolonged dry spells show where the pits for them were dug stand and it is possible the pits were dug but stones never raised in them.

Sarsen Circle

We do not know whether the circle around the horseshoe of trilithons was part of one whole original design or whether it evolved after the trilithons had been erected. Either way, instead of enclosing the horseshoe of trilithons within an earthen mound as had be done by the long barrow builders, it was enfolded within a circle of stones. In other parts of the British Isles, people had built circular monuments, such as Le Dehus in Guernsey, Newgrange in Ireland and, more significantly given that there is evidence of people travelling from the area, Maeshowe in the Orkney Isles. Perhaps the circle represented the horizon in an open landscape, visible from each of the afore mentioned places, and therefore the world. Circular mounds are roughly contemporary with the advent of agriculture - perhaps there was a connection.

Around the horseshoe of trilithons, the original design is traditionally thought to have been for a circle of thirty sarsen uprights capped by thirty sarsen lintels. Thirty is the nearest whole figure to the number of days in a lunar month. One of the uprights is smaller than the others and, if it is the original stone in its original position, would not have supported lintels, making the design an even more accurate twenty nine and a half stones.

If the trilithons represented the moon, perhaps the outer circle of sarsens was erected to represent the sun. The circle of lintels may therefore have represented the sun itself and the sarsens connected it to Earth. In summertime the shadows are close to the stones but in midwinter they stretch as far as the henge, like sun rays.

The lintel stones were shaped to curve round to form a perfect circle on both the inner and outer edges. The uprights are shaped to taper up towards the top. This would have given the impression of perfect symmetry when seen from the centre after completion. The inner surfaces of the stones are very smooth because the monument was meant to be seen from the inside looking out. Although the majority of the shaping and dressing of the stones was done outside of the henge monument, as revealed by chippings in the soil, there may been final finishing once the stones were in place. However, the predominant sound during the building work could well have been of men singing, creating the rhythm to work in unison. Without the benefit of modern day cranes and tools, Neolithic people created an engineering marvel of sophisticated architecture using only the most basic of tools.

Micaceous Sandstone/Altar Stone

A single stone, unique of its type, was set up in the centre of the stone structure. It was a micaceous sandstone whose origins are uncertain but is likely to be from Wales or Cornwall, possibly brought from somewhere along the route traversed with the bluestones. Weighing six and a quarter tons and sixteen feet long, it was considerably larger than the bluestones - although only one cubit thick, (the distance between the elbow and the tip of the middle finger). It could have been transported in the same way as the bluestones.

Freshly cut would have had a surface that was a myriad of reflections. Glitter, body paint and old-fashioned tinsel are made from mica. When the first rays of the rising sun touched it, it would have shone like glass - not so brightly but that sort of effect. It must have had a stunning effect on a superstitious people. It would have been very obviously the centre of the monument, the focal point of the rituals they performed. In other parts of the world and in the Native American Indian tradition, shiny stone - usually quartz - is seen as having properties of transformation and an association with visions. There may be a parallel between the shiny surface of the eye and shiny stone - both are intimately associated with light. There may have been a symbolic connection with light, the sun and supernatural power. Raised from the earth, perhaps it was used to draw power down from the sun.

It was in the centre of the monument. People may even have thought of as being the very centre of the world - in the same way that the Mesolithic posts may have been viewed. A similar claim was made of the oracle stone at Delphi. It may have been known as the Goddess Stone after the Earth Goddess worshipped around this time. It is now known as the Altar Stone. Standing in front of it looking out towards the Heel Stone is the direction of the midsummer solstice sunrise. From the Heel Stone, looking into the centre of the monument, the midwinter solstice sun would have set behind it, framed by the largest trilithon. It seems to have been deliberately placed to lie along the axis created by the midwinter solstice sunrise/midsummer solstice sunset, which is at an 80% angle to the midwinter solstice sunset/midsummer sunrise axis.

Entrance

In addition to the Heel Stone and its companion just outside of the henge bank, two, or possibly three stones stood in the main entrance to the bank itself, between the Heel Stone and the circle of stones.

Removal of Stations Stones

Once the sarsen stage of building was completed, it would no longer have been possible to see the alignments over the Station Stones and it may have been at this time that one of each pair of stones was removed, together with the Heel Stone's partner. By necessity their use then changed but because we have no written tradition in this country we have to look to other cultures to get an idea of what may have been happening here. In the Jewish tradition sacrificial offerings such as sin offerings were made outside the sacred precincts of the temple, something which is described in the building of both the Mosaic tabernacle and the temple of Solomon. The Station Stones may have been sites for similar offerings. The Mosaic tabernacle was built c.1,570 BC, when Stonehenge was complete and in full use. It has been observed by archaeologists that things done by one community are often done at approximately the same time by another community, even when there has been no contact between them.

Rearrangement of Bluestones

The bluestones had been removed from the Aubrey Holes. Perhaps their original purpose had been obscured in the four centuries that had passed since they were first erected. The stone holes were filled in but the people continued to place cremated remains into the infill, persisting perhaps to believe that their ancestors continued to watch over them and care for them even after they had died. The cremations may well have been those of leaders; people who may have been revered as gods during their lifetimes, people who had the knowledge they needed to survive. Although this was a stone circle, timber circles in other places dating to the same period of time are found to have been used subsequently as cremation cemeteries.

Perhaps the sarsen builders had already forgotten why the bluestones had originally been brought, perhaps their oral traditions had been embellished with the importance of the sarsens, in keeping with their enormous size. Perhaps the orientation of their ritual was Skywards instead of Earthwards. However, the bluestones were reintroduced to the structure as a further arrangement inside the sarsen stones, so the effort involved in bringing them could not have been forgotten. We do not know whether this was done as part of the same plan but it would seem there may have been a hiatus between finishing the sarsen structure and this happening. This is because around 2,550 BC, uniquely and without ceremony, a man was buried in a very shallow grave near the entrance to the monument, his head towards the sunrise. He was a young man in his 20's, 5' 10" tall, who had been shot repeatedly with flint arrows in the chest area. He was killed by barbed and tanged arrowheads which were found embedded between his ribs, though not necessarily as a sacrifice. The burial could not have been prior to that date as it took place before the bluestones were in their final position. By the goods buried with him, he had been an archer. By the shape of his skull, he was a member of the Beaker culture, incomers who were not settled in the immediate vicinity at the time he was killed. Who was he? Was he a sacrifice? Or had he perpetrated the inner sanctum of the elite, violating their sacred space?

The bluestones were arranged as a double arc of stones inside the circle of sarsen stones. Over the main axis line to frame the midwinter solstice sunset/midsummer sunrise, bluestones may have been put up as two trilithons, using the tallest of the bluestones. It may originally have been intended to erect a double circle, as pits were dug which never held stones. We do not know how long the bluestones stood like this before being rearranged yet again. In preparation, the bluestones were removed and their holes rammed with chalk.

The bluestones were next rearranged as a circle of fifty-nine inside the sarsen circle. A bluestone oval of nineteen stones was constructed inside the sarsen horseshoe of five trilithons. The oval arrangement included the bluestone trilithons, re-using them as pillars - the mortises can still be seen but the tenons were deliberately battered flat.

They were further rearranged by removing the northern arc of the oval and the stones reused within the remaining horseshoe shape. The stones that were removed may have been used to 'fill in' gaps in the remaining horseshoe. It could have been done to reflect the sarsen horseshoe of trilithons and may have been done centuries, if not millennia, later.

The re-shaping of pillars suggesting they had previously stood as trilithons are not the only ones that appear to have had a different use. One has a 'channel' carved along its length. It is unlikely that this served a use in its current position.

The bluestones are arranged alternately as tall, slim pillars and short, squat blocks, possibly to represent male and female, reflecting the importance of fertility and contributing to the theory that the monument was used around this time as a fertility temple. The white flecked bluestone stood against the light grey of the dressed sarsens. The circle and oval seem to be part of the same plan but this cannot be established without doubt. The bluestones form a rather ragged circle. A circle could have been patterned using a peg and string, but it would not have been possible to use this method once the sarsen structure was in the way.

In addition to the stones previously used in the Aubrey Holes, stones may have been brought from the bluestone circle - West Amesbury henge - which stood at the river end of the Avenue to complete the design. Fifty six had stood in the Aubrey holes and there were twenty seven in the circle by the river. The final arrangement inside the sarsen circle was for a circle of fifty nine and a horseshoe of nineteen.

Astronomical Alignments

With the profound understanding of astronomy that infiltrated their lives, the numbers of stones may have had astronomical significance. Half a millennium earlier, the fifty six Aubrey Holes had been dug perhaps to represent the number of days it takes for the moon to orbit the earth twice. It is also the closest whole number to the number of years in three lunar years, (3 x 18.61), when the moon not only rises in the same position on the horizon with the same pattern of constellations behind it but also in the same phase. One of the sarsen uprights of the outer circle is not tall enough to support a lintel, enforcing the theory that each upright sarsen represents the twenty nine and a half days in a lunar month, from full moon to full moon. Using fifty nine bluestones in a circle inside them could represent the number of days in two lunar months - the number of days between identical moon phases; new moon to new moon or full moon to full moon. The five trilithons could each represent one of the five planets visible with the naked eye from earth. The nineteen bluestones inside of that could represent the number of solar years in a lunar year. The main axis is the invisible line between the midwinter solstice sunset and the midsummer solstice sunrise. The altar stone lies across this but is not at right angles to it. If it was originally positioned to lie at eighty degrees from the main axis line as it appears, rather than ninety degrees for a right angle, it was aligned so the length was along the midwinter solstice sunrise/midsummer sunset line. To further corroborate this, the outer faces of the Great Trilithon appear to be along this line also. There is a notch in one of the uprights of the trilithon to the west of the Great Trilithon, which is aligned to the midwinter solstice sunrise. There is a barrow - which may overlay an earlier feature - from which the midsummer sunrise could be viewed in the window 'box' created by the Great Trilithon rising over the lintels of the outer circle. The various astronomical alignments demonstrate an advanced knowledge acquired through prolonged observation. The knowledge was encoded in stone, so they became a repository of ancient knowledge - but whether this was the purpose for which it was built, or to celebrate it, or for rituals to evolve around, we do not know at this time.

Rituals

The movements of the heavenly bodies feature in myths with no notion of 'worship'. People of the Neolithic are unlikely to have thought their fate was in the hands of ritual specialists - they witnessed first hand the cycles of the seasons. Consequently they had no need of celestial calendars. It may have been that to Neolithic people, they constructed monuments in response to awesome beliefs enshrined in myths, rituals and the terrifying visions of seers. The building of and gathering at such structures would enhance their own prestige.

We can only guess at the kind of ceremonies that may have been undertaken by the builders of Stonehenge and their descendants. We can look to Neolithic sites around the world where there is archaeological evidence leaving clues. We can look at indigenous cultures who have retained a remembrance of ceremonies they have been performing for thousands of years. Rituals had evolved as a result of the ancient understanding and wisdom of the sun, moon and stars and of responsibilities to their ancestors. So the builders of Stonehenge probably had a continued relationship with the dead, which may have included enabling the ancestors to transform into spirit and mediating with the cosmos on their behalf. Their mid winter celebrations may have been joyful celebrations resembling *El Dia de los Muertos,* the Mexican Day of the Dead, a tradition of festivity which recognises death as part of the natural cycle, an opportunity to reunite with those who no longer walk amongst us. We know that people gathered at Durrington Walls for midwinter solstice ceremonies. They may have made their way to Stonehenge by going south along the river, to the beginning of the Avenue, before processing along it to the monument to commune with their revered ancestors. Perhaps they scattered the ashes of their recent dead on the surface of the river - this was at the time when people stopped eating fish, suggesting they had become taboo as a food source, having been in contact with the dead. The river itself may have been seen as an entry to the ancestral

Lowerworld, as rivers were in other parts of the world. The most well known entrance to the Underworld is the river Styx of Greek mythology.

There is likely to have been an acknowledgement of the sun, moon and stars that had always been important to them. The numbers of stones used in the design could have codified the cosmic order, which causes the cyclical change of life and death. They may have appealed for animals to thrive and for crops to grow. Their awareness of the cosmos coupled with care and respect of the living Earth that provided them with all their needs - the Mother who nurtured them beyond the capabilities of a biological mother - crystallised into ceremony. Early agrarian cultures were strongly aware of the cyclical order of the seasons, a constant renewal, a concept of eternal return. Their myths, monuments and ways of living related to it. Their ceremonies may have evolved to support the fields and meadows, the animals and the people with vital forces and creative power.

Eventually gatherings held ceremonies believed to be of life and death importance, to please or placate or even to manipulate the spirits that cohabited their world. People impelled and implored what could not be controlled but that was needed for survival with aids such as imitation magic. Rites developed into rituals that were repeated by rote, performed without necessarily understanding them.

Life at Durrington Walls

When the sarsen construction at Stonehenge had been completed, more dwellings were built, used seasonally or at celebrations - almost Bronze Age hotels. It implies something of social or symbolic use rather than a practical need for shelter. There were eventually around 1,000 of them, sheltering approximately 4,000 people. Between 2,500 - 2,460 BC it was the largest settlement anywhere in northwest Europe. The dwellings built on the highest land, commanding the best view, were possibly for people of a higher status. There may have been a powerful person or family controlling the resources of the area. One structure was sufficiently impressive to suggest that it belonged to a leading family whose food was brought to them from a cooking area elsewhere as there are no signs of domestic activity such as cooking, despite the central fireplace. Alternately, it may have been used ritually, to communicate with the ancestors. It is now called the Western Enclosure.

The floors of the houses were excavated for organic matter, such as cereal. There was so little that it would appear they were occupied largely only seasonally. Very few domestic tools have been found and no quern stones for grinding cereal. Broken pottery has been found. People probably came from the Southampton area and the Somerset levels, meeting on neutral territory. Cattle teeth have been found in middens and testing for strontium 90 - the substance indicating the precise locality of the water drunk by the animals when they were young - shows the animals were not brought up in the locality but in Devon and Cornwall, Wales and the Orkney Isles in Scotland. The latter was a month's walk each way. People bringing them contributed them to the feasting celebrations, others were bartered to improve their stock.

Flints were used not only as a huge variety of weaponry but also as tools to prepare meat and other domestic uses and as knives to skin and cure animal hides for clothing. Stone axes were still used not only to cut trees down in order to build houses but for other items made from wood. With the use of stone and flint tools, items such as bows were fashioned, clubs in imitation of antlers, pins for clothes, tubs and buckets and boats were built. Joinery skills were very limited, just notches and holes in planks through which round stakes were driven.

Food consisted of grains, berries, fish and leaves such as stinging nettles, fat hen, orache, white dead nettle and cleavers used as vegetables. Flavouring may have been provided with Jack-by-the-hedge, ransomes, biting stonecrop, lady's smock, (peppery), sorrel, (lemony), salad burnet, (cucumbery), mints and juniper berries. Stews, soups and porridge were cooked with a variety of these. Cereal was used to make some sort of bread and also beer. Cider was probably an accidental discovery which would have occurred spontaneously with harvested crab apples. Mead - fermented honey - was flavoured with meadowsweet and lime. The yeast that occurs naturally in honey may have been used as a source when brewing ale. Some of the plants that grew nearby were useful additions to the diet and some useful for animals feed. Tubers, such as pignut could be boiled, dried, cooked, baked and served like potatoes. They gathered fruits such as crab apples, sloes, blackberries, hips and haws. Acorns do not appear to have been eaten but were ritually burned. Some plants may have been used for medicinal use. Bracken may have been used for animal bedding and fertilizer or a mulch to dampen weed growth. Poppies could have been grown or gathered and crushed to make oil, for flavouring or for medicinal use and the leaves used to feed animals. Meat was reserved for feasting and ceremonies rather than included on the everyday menu. They cooked it by roasting, boiling or wrapping it in clay, straw or dough to bake it directly in the fire or in stone cooking pits. Pigs were hunted but later domesticated as is shown by changes in the teeth found, caused by change in their diet. Pork seems to have been eaten as a treat at times of celebration. Finds indicate they were kept, fattened and then killed at specific times of the year, times when the people gathered. Some pig teeth were rotten, suggesting the animals were deliberately sweetened and fattened. Large quantities of eight month old pig was eaten indicating that the major gathering time was midwinter. The meat was roasted and bones thrown away when still attached by sinew, which is a way of eating during feasting. Midwinter celebrations were possibly centred on ancestor worship. Durrington Walls may have been used for ceremonies in connection with Stonehenge, the theory being that the timber monuments were connected with the living and the stones with the dead, the ancestors. Fish disappeared from the diet. If the river had become integral to deposition of the dead not of high enough status to warrant ritual interment, then it perhaps became taboo and creatures that lived in it unclean to eat. Similar ideas may have existed about animals that fed on carrion such as wolves, foxes and some birds. Or they may just not have tasted as good as domestic animals.

Red deer, roe deer, aurochs and wolf continued to roam. Animals they domesticated were cattle, sheep, pigs and dogs, possibly goats. These animals would have needed water, food through grazing but possibly supplemented. Winters caused food shortage and seasonal stress so they may have provided winter housing for them. They needed protection from scavengers, particularly when young, as there were wolves, bears, wildcat and raptors such as red kite and ravens. They may have needed to protect their female stock from interbreeding with wild animals - cattle from aurochs, pig from wild boar and dogs from wolves - which would have resulted in difficult pregnancy and birth and undesirable traits in the offspring. Dogs had been kept since Mesolithic times from medium to large in size, fed on scavenged bone and kept as hunting animals. Cats were probably not kept as pets but appeared as predators. Cattle were introduced from Europe, not bred from auroch. They were approximately 1.2 metres at the shoulder with short horns and probably hairy. They were used for meat, possibly traction, for dairy - milk and, it can be assumed, cheese such as cottage cheese and for by-products like leather. Sheep may have been similar to feral soay sheep. They were possibly given winter shelter and for lambing. They may have been kept for meat, milk and skin. One by-product unique to Britain was wool, although Neolithic sheep's wool was hairier than modern wool. Some sheep moult and were plucked rather than shorn. As time went by, there was an increase in pig numbers over cattle. Down by the river were otter, beaver, mallard and cormorant and in the woodland foxes, badgers and woodcock. Hares may have lived on the open downland.

Fabric was woven from plant fibres. One of the most readily available was nettle fibres which could be woven into a coarse linen look cloth. By dyeing it with plant dyes before weaving plaid effect patterns could be produced. Indigotin produced blue, luteolin and apigenin yellow and red dye possibly came from red madder. Nettle fibres were also used for string and rope. Bone combs and tweezers have also been found, plant extracts may have been used for 'war paint' and make up. It is possible that hair was sometimes woven into elaborate styles. There may have bead decorated head gear, belted tunics, outer cloaks, leggings and shoes. There was some difference between men and women's clothing. Jewellery could be anything from a stone with a hole in it threaded onto string to gold and gem stones.

People are likely to have been aware of the medicinal properties of plants in order to care for their sick or injured. They certainly performed surgery. Trepanation was a surgical procedure whereby a skin flap was cut to reveal the skull in order to then bore into the bone using flint knives. It was used from Neolithic times onwards, probably to relieve headache, for epilepsy and for mental illness. There was a 50% survival rate. There are rare instances of osteoporosis, probably because people died before reaching age related disorders. Acute infectious diseases were probably the most common cause of death. There is no sign of diseases such as tuberculosis, leprosy or syphilis, all of which leave signs on bone. Food took more chewing and teeth were stronger but ground down with use. Lack of sugar in their diet left them intact.

Decorative pots were made from clay and fired in open fires. Some were for domestic use, some funerary. They were decorated with small bones, such as bird bones, plants or simple thumb nail prints.

They continued to tell their stories. Social groups define themselves by their myth. Mythology constructs a framework that wells up from the human consciousness and the struggles to make sense of it. Neurological experiences had led to ritual practises which in turn were designed to induce experience of vision, ecstasy. Eventually monuments were built whose purpose may have included preparing the mind for such experience. By guiding what was seen and discrediting originality and individuality that challenged the authority of ritual specialists, they would have become increasingly powerful.

Between 2,480 - 2,460 BC a henge, a huge bank and ditch was built around the buildings, most probably as a closing deposit when the site was abandoned. It enclosed 12 hectares, making it the second largest henge in terms of area in the country. The bank was 30 metres high and 30 metres wide and would, created as it was from white chalk, have stood out for miles on the landscape. Part of it, north and west, crests a natural chalk scarp. Sixty stones flanked the southern bank, (although they may have preceded it). The main entrance faces the midwinter sunrise along the avenue and is marked by a huge tree post, a metre in diameter. A tree of that size must have come from either the Savernake Forest, twenty miles north or the New Forest area, twenty miles south. There is another entrance aligned to the midsummer sunset. Building the henge must have been instigated by an incredibly powerful person who could organise a vast labour force.

Although the henge had been built over some of the houses, the central area continued to be used. About 2,400 BC a new style of pottery started to be deposited, a style called Beaker pottery. The pottery is sufficiently distinctive that the culture who made them have been named the Beaker people after them. The Beaker people arrived in Britain about 2,500 and brought with them not only their distinctive pottery but also weaponry and ornamentation, new ideas and culture. This may have led to them becoming the hierarchy amongst the indigenous population. One might expect these newcomers to aim for the most important area in the country but initially their presence did not encroach and was in a wide area circling Salisbury Plain, suggesting that the indigenous population did not integrate with them, kept them away, that they did not welcome the newcomers and that they were strong enough and well organised enough to enforce this.

Woodhenge

Just outside of the henge to the south is largest of the ceremonial timber circles, Woodhenge. It was built around 2,300 BC, after Durrington Walls had been abandoned. Like the Southern Circle, it consists of six concentric oval rings of posts which had once held timber posts, measuring 43 x 40 metres. The overall diameter of the henge is of 110 metres. It has one entrance to the north east and, like Stonehenge, is aligned to the midsummer sunrise.

The timbers decayed in situ. It was probably after this that four sarsen stones less than 2 metres high were set up in the south of the circle. They formed a three sided setting opening to the west. In turn, these were removed and replaced by two large sarsen stones, probably more than 2 metres high.

Cuckoo Stone

To the west of Woodhenge lies a single sarsen stone. This stone was raised upright in its own socket hole, in the same way the Heel Stone had been raised, with a possible date of 2,900 BC. It may have indicated the route across the landscape from Durrington Walls to Stonehenge. The axis of the Cursus runs through it and Woodhenge in the direction of the highest land to the east.

During the Bronze Age people brought the ashes of their dead in former cooking pots to bury next to the stone.

Bronze Age Burial mounds 2,500 BC

Rising of a society

All around the landscape at Stonehenge there are humps and bumps that can be seen in the ground and these are round barrows. They were evolving monuments, starting with one use - most likely ritual - and the majority later used as burial mounds. This is the function for which they are best known - burial mounds with a primary burial of just one person. A grave was dug and the deceased placed in it in the foetal position, perhaps in preparation for rebirth into the Afterlife - so as both foetus and corpse. Around were placed grave goods. Over this, a cave-like structure of wood - or stone in other areas where there was a ready supply - was erected. Over this soil was heaped, creating huge mounds. Some of them have later secondary burials or cremations buried in the mound. There are four main types of barrow - bell, bowl, pond and disc-shaped. Pond shaped ones are depressions in the ground. Disc ones are circular, with a circular bank around a central small mound. Bowl ones are huge mounds surrounded by a ditch. The most complex ones are the bell shaped ones which have a berm around them enclosed by a ditch. They tend to contain the richest graves and belong to the later elite.

There is a hiatus in burial style between the building of long barrows and round barrows. Some round barrows were built over the top of miniature long barrows intended for single burial and these may be the intermediary burial style for a few elite.

Barrows were built in cemetery groups rather than single burial sites. It was style of burial used throughout the building and use of the stone phases of Stonehenge, a period lasting just over a thousand years from 2,660 - 1,550 BC. They were built not only to be visible from Stonehenge but also to overlook it and would have stood out on the landscape in gleaming white chalk. They may been deliberately kept clear of grass and vegetation, not covered in grass and bushes as they are now. The very last ones to be built were created from turfs, rather than mounded over with chalk, for which several acres of grassland would have been needed. It is possible that the deliberate turfing, which left the soil exposed, gave rise to the Celtic field systems which surround but do not encroach on the burial mounds.

It was only the very most important people - the equivalent of kings and leaders - who were buried in this way, usually one primary burial in each barrow, so in effect the area surrounding Stonehenge is England's answer to Egypt's Valley of the Kings. In the three mile radius around Stonehenge, there are 490 of them, so this is all part of a very sacred and spiritual landscape, with Stonehenge itself the jewel in the crown of that landscape.

We glean a little of what was significant to these people by the things they considered important enough to be buried with. The grave goods included pottery, weapons, tools and jewellery - things they had used in this life and would need to survive in the next. Most have distinctive pottery drinking vessels, beakers, introduced into this country by people named after their distinctive pottery, the Beaker people. They evolved into the rich and powerful society we now know as the Wessex Culture, the predominant culture in the area of the monument and associated with its use. Included in the repetitive designs are zigzags, seen in cave painting as trance images and a link to the shamanic world. Armoury and weapons such as axes and daggers were deposited. Tools of a lifetime's trade have been found, craftsmen's tools and farming implements. Jewellery included shale from the coasts, amber and jet from Scandinavia and blue faience beads from Egypt. These would have been passed along trade routes together with stories, histories and ideas. More faience beads have been found in Wiltshire than in the rest of England, Scotland, Wales, Brittany, Holland and Spain put together. The jewellery was found by female burials, women buried in these prestigious graves - which proves that women could be important and powerful. Other jewellery include pendants - amber set in gold, a miniature halberd, double headed axes - and ear studs and labrets. Members of the elite may have been sent into the Afterlife to communicate with the gods and ancestors and to safeguard the well-being of the living, adorned with auspicious and magical symbols of power. Items such as these were made from jadeite, eclogite and omphiate - heirlooms perhaps hundreds of years old before they were deposited may have been sacred treasures of an individual or of the community. Stories of the individuals themselves - heros, warriors, chiefs, shamans - would surely have been woven into the fabric of their oral traditions and sagas.

The Boscombe Bowmen were seven individuals buried together in one normal sized grave with pottery and arrowheads. Burials of this time usually contained one or possibly two skeletons. There were three men, probably related, a male teenager and three children, almost certainly originating from Wales. One of them had a major trauma to his thigh, suggestive of a huge impact consistent with having a stone fall on him. Perhaps he had been in an accident when moving a bluestones. However, despite limited medical resources, he survived.

The occupant of one barrow in the Normanton Down group, south of Stonehenge, has become known as the 'bush barrow warrior'. The barrow is in an important position in relation to the monument, being in line with it and the midwinter sunset. The grave goods were the belongings of a very rich man, who lived 1,900 - 1,700 BC. He was about 1.83 metres tall - the average height of a bronze age man from those in the burial mounds was 1.72 metres and women averaged 1.61 metres. The grave goods included a gold-decorated helmet, gold-embellished daggers, a gold button cover and a jadeite mace of office. He also has what has traditionally been interpreted as a gold shield, a symbolic one, as gold is too soft to be functional. It is a gold lozenge with 80% angles - the same angle as the midwinter solstice sunrise/midsummer solstice sunset axis is to the midsummer solstice sunrise/midwinter sunset axis. Perhaps, therefore, it was portable information, depicting these angles.

Bush barrow is by far the richest barrow investigated. The builders of Stonehenge people used gold as a sign of prestige, for decoration on armoury - on helmets, shields and particularly in decorating daggers. This is known as gold pontille work, a method of driving minuscule gold rivets into a dagger to decorate it. Within the grave were an estimated 140,000 of them. The gold probably came from Ireland. He also had copper and bronze artefacts with him. All are prestige items and much of the gold found in barrows is displayed in Devizes museum, Wiltshire.

Another internment, three miles south-east of Stonehenge, dubbed the Amesbury Archer, was the burial of a high ranking individual. He had a huge array of about 100 grave goods, including pottery, flint arrowheads suggestive of a quiver full of arrows, archer's wrist guard to protect him from the bowstring, three copper knives - one of Spanish origin - a metal workers' cushion stone and two small gold hair tresses. It is likely that the items were placed in the Archer's grave for his use in the Afterlife. He had everything he would need - clothing, tools, weapons, pottery. The burial dated to about 2,300 BC. He was 35 - 45 years of age and had grown up in the Alps. He may have travelled widely through central and western Europe and brought the 'magical' skill of metalworking to Britain, as he was one of the earliest metalworkers in the country. He had a powerful build but there was an abscess on his jaw and a few years before his death he had an accident which ripped his left knee cap off. This meant he would have walked with his left leg straight out to the side. He also had an infection in his bones which would have left him in constant pain. If Stonehenge had remained renowned for the healing properties of its stones, perhaps this is what brought him to the area.

Close to him was a second skeleton, belonging to a man aged 25 - 30, whose early childhood was spent in Wessex and then travelled, possibly with the Amesbury Archer. His foot bones suggest that he may have been from the same family, perhaps father and son. He had grown up in southern England but travelled in the Midlands or north-east Scotland in his late teenage years. He had a pair of gold hair tresses like those of the Amesbury Archer, for some reason placed in his mouth.

At Bulford, a short distance east from Durrington Walls, was a burial with grave goods that suggested the occupant had status as a shaman.

On the south west edge of the three mile radius is a group of barrows known as the Winterbourne Stoke group. The round barrows were built around a single long barrow built 600 years before the circular bank at Stonehenge. This is the one that contained the body of just one man rather than being used as a communal burial site. It would seem he was remembered in oral traditions because a millennium after his burial a group of barrows were ranged nearby, as though the Bronze Age burials were trying to absorb something of his potency in order to add to their own prestige. It is a particularly important group because it contains each different type of round barrow - bell, bowl, pond and disc shaped mounds. There is evidence of a farmstead nearby belonging to this period - a cluster of small wooden huts which were very probably thatched. Not far from this the Wilsford Shaft, a shaft 100 feet deep in the ground. In the bottom layers was a strange assortment of artefacts, including broken pottery, wooden buckets and bits of cord, suggesting that water extraction was undertaken in the Bronze Age. Additionally, it could have been dug as a shaft to the Lowerworld and the artefacts arrived at its base as offerings and libations.

This all goes to demonstrate that the whole landscape around Stonehenge had become sacred and spiritual. A ritual landscape. People did not live there, they settled outside of the sacred area at Durington Walls and Blick Mead.

Blick Mead had remained special throughout the millennia, a place that people returned to and left objects they had crafted. At some time during the Bronze Age, two little ducks carved from chalk were deposited in the spring. They are the oldest figurines found in Britain and Ireland. In Brittany there was a goddess of healing and fertility, Sequana, (also an early name for the River Seine), whose shape shifted into that of a duck. That a duck could swim and then take flight may well have been magical - embodying the healing properties of water by swimming on it and taking flight to avoid the hunters' arrow.

Another later deposit was a piece of a copper alloy dagger, decorated with a chevron pattern. It was probably ceremonial rather than functional. It had been made from a Bronze Age rapier, possibly because it had broken and was sufficiently valued that the point was kept and made into a dagger. Taking the trouble to preserve it suggests it was important to those who owned it. A Bronze Age chisel was also deposited, so that by around 1,400 BC the spring may have been used to ritually deposit weapons.

Carvings

There are carvings on many of the sarsen stones. The majority of them are axe head carvings of the early Bronze Age, signifying an axe cult at that stage. An axe head was the symbol that represented the female Mother Goddess or her aspect as Guardian of the Dead - the dead who watched over and safeguarded them. The Mother Goddess represented the living earth and may have been worshiped as a mother who nurtures and nurses her children, who in turn cared for her. Early agrarian cultures were very aware of the cyclical order of the seasons and the concept of the eternal return, something that appears repeatedly in early mythology.

The axe carvings are on a stones which have significant positions, such as at the entrance, rather than having been carved at random. The stones had already been standing for seven hundred years when they were carved, indicating that people continued to gather at the monument. They cover the lower face of one which overlooks the central and focal point of the monument, the Altar Stone, much as a cross is placed in a Christian church to overlook the altar. On that same one is a dagger carving. It may have been a life-size carving of a local weapon, belonging to a leader of the society who used Stonehenge, the dagger that was indicative of his power and wealth. It would have been an object of prestige, like a mace of office, rather than a functional item. Only a very skilled craftsman could have produced this beautiful object, perhaps embellished it with magical, mystical qualities and no doubt his renown as a craftsman would have travelled far and wide, with story tellers telling of him as they travelled along trade routes. These trade routes may well have extended as far as the Greek islands.

On one of the islands, Mycenae, sheep grazed on the rich grass of the island and produced fine, soft fleeces, almost golden in colour. These fleeces were a very desirable commodity and maybe tradesmen from Salisbury Plain exchanged gold pontille work daggers for the fine fleeces. Perhaps it is then not too much to speculate that the leader of the society that built Stonehenge protected himself from the elements of the land - which according to the Greeks was beyond the North Wind - in cloth woven from wool that had grown on the backs of sheep in Mycenae. The daggers exchanged subsequently became the symbol of the Mycenaen civilisation, which was developing at the time when Stonehenge was completed and in full use, (Mycenaen civilisation flourished circa 1,600 -1,200 BC). There are many dagger carvings of this type in the Greeks islands but it is most unusual to find this type of carving outside of them. Furthermore, the postern gate at Mycenae is distinctively similar in design to a trilithon of Stonehenge.

There is another carving, reputedly the symbol of the Mother Goddess. It is so high up that it is unlikely that it was carved once the stone was raised upright. This particular one is a stone that has fallen and been raised, so the carving is not necessarily prehistoric. Similar carvings have been found on stones in Brittany and the Stonehenge people seem to have had a number of links with Brittany - including the fact that similar weapons were used at the same period - suggesting that its leader(s) had spent time there, perhaps brought up there. Again the stone overlooks what was probably the focal point during ritual worship. The carving is representative rather than symbolistic and difficult to decipher. Its authenticity is questionable. It cannot be seen from outside the stone circle.

In 3rd millennium BC, portable art in the form of two carved chalk plaques were deposited on the King Barrow Ridge overlooking Stonehenge, one of which was carved with a geometric pattern which could be interpreted as neurological imagery. The other looks remarkably like a rough etching of trilithons. Perhaps a Neolithic souvenir? They are on display in the Stonehenge visitors' centre.

The Avenue
1,900 BC

Stonehenge stood in the centre of the landscape, its vast stones surrounded by a decaying circular chalk bank. In the three mile radius around it, there were over 500 mounds - fifteen of which were long barrows and the remainder round barrows. The areas cleared of turf to construct some of them might have stood out as white areas around the barrows, while the barrows themselves capped with chalk would also have stood out white in the landscape. North of the monument was the Cursus, now partly silted up and decayed, with vegetation covering its chalk banks.

When the people wanted to go into the monument for their various festivities and ceremonies, they climbed the slope from the river, through the sacred landscape, along the high ridge of land passing the resting places of their ancestors, maybe telling stories of them as they went along. Perhaps they also performed rituals at some of the structures around the landscape. The route dropped down into a coomb before curving up a slope to the stones. Perhaps this was a gathering point because from the coomb the stones are invisible. Within few yards, the stones rise monumentally, suddenly, very immediately. The natural landscape may have been deliberately used to best theatrical effect.

The last element in the sequence of construction was to build twin parallel banks with a quarry ditch on the outside of each all along this route, enclosing some of the periglacial soil stripes that may have been significant since the earliest awareness of the area. It is now called the Avenue. The building of this, although difficult to date, seems to belong to the very last phase of building and was possibly built as a folk memory of the old ceremonial way along which the bluestones had been carried. It is unlikely to post-date 1,900 BC. In the words of Richard Atkinson, who began investigating Stonehenge in the 1950's, 'it appears to be a processional way linking Stonehenge with the River Avon and ... its inception may have had something to do with the hauling of the bluestones from the river to the monument.' Close to its termination at the entrance to Stonehenge stood the Heel Stone, surrounded by a ring ditch. The line of the Avenue changes direction to accommodate it.

Midsummer - Heelstone from the Avenue

Y and Z Holes

People continued to use the monument. Evidence suggests further building had been planned as two circles of holes, known as Y and Z holes, were dug outside of the sarsen circle, (1,700 - 1,500 B.C.), and probably never used. However, they prove that activity continued on the site. After that, although there was no further building, people are likely to have remained aware of the site - at least through their oral traditions - and probably continued to gather there, perhaps in reduced numbers.

We do not know the purpose of the holes or whether they were intended to hold markers such as timber posts. Were they intended to form a kind of labyrinth? Walking through labyrinths has long been known to induce trance needed to journey to Otherworlds. If this was the intention, it would imply that the people who dug them were following a long tradition of shamanic activity on the site.

A Few Last Thoughts…

If we could converse with the builders of Stonehenge, would we be able to understand their concepts? Would we be able to see with their thoughts? We would be able to understand their emotions - their sense of awe, wonder and terror - but we cannot know what they were in response to.

When they built Stonehenge, were they expressing something that is hard wired into the human neurological system? Is that what we still recognise? If the design derives from something deep in the neurological hard wiring, whatever it represents, it resonates within us, even if it undergoes varying interpretation as we strive to make sense of it. In none of its stages of building is Stonehenge typical of contemporary constructions, so it has been unique throughout its history. The question remains as to why Neolithic farmers should use precious resources to build the monument, successfully combining simplicity of design with multiplicity of purpose. From the time when the circular bank had been dug to the time when the stones were raised in their final arrangement in the centre, a total period of eight hundred years had passed. The ideas and influences of many different generations were incorporated into its design during that time. By 1,500 BC activity on the site was waning. Shortly after, the monument began to go out of use. Had the first stone fallen indicating the displeasure of the gods?

Stonehenge survives in the present as link with the past. Within those silent portals is a mystery to challenge the human imagination, a space for awe and wonder.

PART THREE

Legendary Stonehenge

The Greeks

Traditionally, Western civilization 'begins' with the Greeks. However, it didn't spring up in a single generation. Social organisation, philosophy, mathematics, literature, architecture, astronomy had developed over centuries, over millennia, orchestrated by descendants of the Stonehenge builders. We can surmise trade links through the dagger carvings. It is within Greek literature we find the first possible references to Stonehenge, through which we can look back at Stonehenge through their eyes, see how they interpreted witness of how it was being used just a few centuries after it was built.

When Homer was writing C8th BC, some people think he may just possibly have patterned his Shield of Achilles with the design of Stonehenge.

"There shone the mirrored Master Mind,
There earth, there sky, there ocean, he designed;
The unwearied Sun, the moon completely round,
The starry lights that the ethereal convex crowned:
The Pleiades, Hyads, with the Northern Team,
And Great Orion's more refulgent beam:
To which, around the Axle of the Sky,
The Bear, revolving, reveals his golden eye,
And shines exalted on the Ethereal Plain,
Nor bathes his blazing forehead in the Main."

Vulcan finished the design with a depiction of the round Earth and the dome of the sky:

"The Broad Shield complete, the Artist Crowned,
With his last hand, he poured the Ocean round."
Iliad XVIII

It is through the Greeks that we have a description that is perhaps Stonehenge. A mariner by the name of Pytheas of Massilia came to Britain around 325 BC and left an account of his travels, fragments of which we have inherited through the writings of later authors. Pytheas witnessed ceremonies performed and recognised the god that was honoured as the sun god, calling him by the Greek name of Apollo rather than by whatever name he was known in Britain. He thereby not only gives us the first written eye witness account but is also interpreting what he saw through the eyes of the society he lived in, something that has been continued throughout the generations since. However, we do not know for certain whether the ceremonies he saw were performed at Stonehenge.

Hecataeus of Abdera wrote in C4th BC, quoting Pytheas, of "an island over against Gaul - its inhabitants called hyperboreans, (beyond the North Wind). "And there is also on the island both a magnificent sacred precinct of Apollo and a notable temple decorated with many offerings…spherical in shape and a city is there which is sacred to this god in which the harpers sing sacred songs to the God from the vernal equinox to the rising of the Pleaides - that once in nineteen years the God appears amidst dancing and playing of the harp." The later refers to the Metonic cycle, the period of all heavenly bodies to return to their exact same positions in the heavens, occurring every 18.61 years. If this account relates to Stonehenge, then it is describing not only the monument but also the 'city', which could be the habitation that had grown up around Blick Mead.

When Diodorus Siculus was writing in C1st BC he quoted ancient accounts:

"Of those who have written about the ancient myths, Hecateus and certain others say that in the regions beyond the land of the Celts, (Gaul), there lies in the ocean an island no smaller than Sicily. This island, the account continues, is situated in the north, and is inhabited by the Hyperboreans, who are called by that name because their home is beyond the point whence the north wind blows…" He continued, "Moreover, the following legend is told concerning it: Leto was born on this island, and for that reason Apollon is honoured among them above all other gods; and the inhabitants are looked upon as priests of Apollon, after a manner, since daily they praise this god continuously in song and honour him exceedingly. And there is also on the island both a magnificent sacred precinct of Apollon and a notable temple which is adorned with many votive offerings and is spherical in shape.... the god visits the island every 19 years, the period in which the return of the stars to the same place in the heavens is accomplished; and for this reason the 18.61-year period is called by the Greeks the year of Mcton."

Leto, reputedly herself from Hyperbora, was the mother of Apollo and his twin sister Artemis, who was representative of the moon. This may have been a way of describing the fact that cosmic events were recorded and predicted within the design of Stonehenge.

Iron Age
800 BC - 43 AD

People continued to travel between Europe and Britain, trading and bringing new ideas and craftsmanship influenced by developing cultures on the continent. Around 600 BC, there is evidence of the first significant use of iron for tools and weapons in Britain. Use of iron succeeded bronze, meaning much harder weapons and tools could be made.

During the Late Bronze Age, new farming ideas influenced the way the land was used. The building of round barrows during the Bronze Age had meant acres of grassland were stripped bare, leaving exposed earth in which to sow seed. This developed into field systems which exploited the land further during the Iron Age. On lowlands there were still farmsteads and villages. Durrington Walls was used by Iron Age farmers 2,000 years after the first houses were built there.

The organizational and monument building skills developed through the Mesolithic and Neolithic Ages were directed towards building territorial markers, such as immense ditches many miles long, indicating the desire to control large areas of land. They also started to build hill forts, single earthwork banks around a natural hill. The development of hill forts may have been a result of tensions that arose between social and tribal groups. We now call the peoples of the many tribes occupying Britain, who spoke a vaguely common language, the Celts. As well as defensive purposes, hill forts were used for domestic purposes, where food was stored, where people lived and craftsmen worked - although this may not have been permanent settlement. By the late Iron Age, they may also have been developing as a result of the accumulation of wealth and a higher standard of living, being used for markets and social contact, perhaps as a development of the way causewayed enclosures had been used 3,000 years earlier.

People of the Iron Age had a structured society and organisational skills, artistic skills, oral literature and poetry. All of which had evolved from the practises of their ancestors. Celtic mythology was an oral, ancestral tradition, telling of the spirits of all in their world. This followed existing, ancient shamanic ideas that all things have a spirit, an essence. The Celts had a wide pantheon of deities. Rituals involved offerings and sacrifices, usually animals. It is generally considered that worship was practised in the open air in natural settings. Springs remained sacred places, linked to goddesses, so Blick Mead would have remained important. Stonehenge had always been an important place so although no further building was done, it is highly likely that it continued to be used locally if not as extensively as it had been during the Bronze Age. During the Iron Age a young adult male who had lived locally was shot from behind with arrowheads, one of which pierced his heart. He was probably shot at close range, suggestive of a sacrifice. He was buried a short distance north west of the henge, with his head towards the east, in a semi-flexed position and lying on his right side.

The Celts followed a practice of placing sick children on healing stones, so the connection with healing continued. In Celtic *main ambres* were anointed, consecrated stones. As the name of the nearby town of Amesbury - the town which developed from the settlement at Blick Mead - would seem to have a similar root, it seems feasible that it may have been known as 'the town of the sacred stones'.

The Druids

The Druids came to Britain from Gaul, now France, during the Iron Age, about 500 BC - two thousand years after Stonehenge had been built. They supposedly came to learn the craft of priesthood from the Celts who were already here and reputedly learnt the ideology of their British teachers. Across the other side of the world in China at the same time as the Druids were arriving in Britain, Confucius was voicing his philosophies. The prophets of the Old Testament lived around this time too. Legend suggests that the hierarchy of the social system of the Celts were prophets, priests and poets - again things connected strongly to the Druids, who are sometimes referred to as the priesthood of the Celts. They may well have become their leaders because of their knowledge and how to use it to hold power over uneducated people. Art depicts them as tall men in flowing white robes, with long beards which is rather reminiscent of Viracocha, Osiris and Quetzalcoatl, legendary leaders of ancient civilisations of the Andes, Egypt and Mexico.

Like the Celts, Druids preferred groves of trees and running water so they did not necessarily use a man-made structure such as Stonehenge to worship in. They had an oral tradition which it took up to twenty years to learn word perfect. Somewhere within that was almost certainly the history of Stonehenge and the reason why it was built, the motivation behind its building.

The Romans

The Romans came to Britain in 43AD, proving the Iron Age hill forts ineffective against their attack. One of the reasons they were interested in coming to the island was in order to grow crops to feed their armies in Europe and they needed the local people to work for them. Salisbury Plain was particularly conducive to growing crops. There are Roman roads/tracks criss-crossing the Plain. Around five miles from Stonehenge, the Iron Age hill fort of Yarnbury Castle was used to store grain before being transported to the coast and shipped across the channel. There are remains of villages, farmsteads and villas across the Plain.

Julius Caesar, (100 - 44 BC), and other Roman writers told of a Celtic priesthood. Caesar's texts tell us that the priests of Britain were Druids, a religious elite with considerable holy and secular powers. The following is a translation of his writings and gives us his view of life in Gaul, which, as the Druids feature predominantly, was probably very similar to life in Britain. Britain had allegedly become the seat of the Druids by this time.

"...Reports say that in the schools of the druids, they learn by heart a great number of verses, and therefore some persons remain twenty years under training. And they do not think it proper to commit these utterances to writing, although in almost all other matters, and in their public and private accounts, they make use of Greek letters. I believe that they have adopted the practice for two reasons: that they do not wish the rule to become common property, nor those who learn the rule to rely on writing and so neglect the cultivation of the memory; and in fact it does usually happen that the assistance of writing tends to relax the diligence of the student and the action of the memory.

"The cardinal doctrine which they seek to teach is that souls do not die, but after death pass from one to another; and this belief they hold to be the greatest incentive to valor, as the fear of death is thereby cast aside. Besides this, they have many discussions as touching the stars and their movement, the size of the universe and of the earth, the order of nature, the strength and the powers of the immortal gods, and hand down their lore to the young men.

"The whole nation of the Gauls is greatly devoted to ritual observances, and for that reason those who are smitten with the more grievous maladies and who are engaged in the perils of battle either sacrifice human victims or vow to do so, employing the druids as ministers for such sacrifices. They believe, in effect, that, unless for a man's life a man's life be paid, the majesty of the immortal gods may not be appeased; and in public, as in private, life they observe an ordinance of sacrifices of the same kind. Others use figures of immense size, whose limbs, woven out of twigs, they fill with living men and set on fire, and the men perish in a sheet of flame. They believe that the execution of those who have been caught in the act of theft or robbery or some crime is more pleasing to the immortal gods; but when the supply of such fails they resort to the execution even of
the innocent.

"Among the gods, they most worship Mercury, (the Roman god who was equivalent to the Celtic deity Lugh). There are numerous images of him; they declare him to be the inventor of all arts, the guide for every road and journey, and they deem him to have the greatest influence for all money-making and traffic. After him they set Apollo, Mars, Jupiter, and Minerva. Of these deities they have almost the same idea as all other nations: Apollo drives away diseases, Minerva supplies the first principles of arts and crafts. Jupiter holds the empire of heaven; Mars controls wars.

"The Gauls affirm that they are all descended from a common father, Dis, (Roman god of the Underworld), and say that this is the tradition of the druids. For that reason they determine all periods of time by the number, not of days, but of nights, and in their observance of birthdays and the beginnings of months and years day follows night."

Extracts Caesar *The Gallic War* VI.14-18

Caesar mentioned that the Celts believed they were the descendants of an ancestor god named Dis. This implies that honouring the ancestors was still important and certainly the ancestors could be appealed to for assistance before battle.

Belief that the Druids performed human sacrifice may have erroneously come from interpretation of shamanic rituals. Across the world shamanic journeys are compared to death and rebirth, as the spirit - or part of it - leaves the physical body for a while. This may have been misunderstood by the Romans, who performed sacrifice as part of their rituals.

The Romans did not like the Druids. They were extremely knowledgeable and knowledge is power. Accusing them of strange rituals including human sacrifice, the Romans killed them and smashed their sacred groves, as Suetonius tells us in his *The Lives of the Caesars - Claudius* XXV.5.

"He (Claudius) utterly abolished the cruel and inhuman religion of the Druids among the Gauls, which under Augustus had merely been prohibited to Roman citizens; ..."

However, in killing them they also killed their oral tradition and perhaps our last chance of understanding the motivation behind the building of Stonehenge. Smashing the Druids venerated places as they did provides another reason to suppose the Druids did not worship at the site. If the Romans had thought they did, it is likely that they would have smashed the stone circle down - and they had the technology to do so. Instead, they may have used it as a temple to their sun god Apollo, suggesting they were following a tradition of veneration to the sun on the site, as was their custom. The Romans adopted practises of local worship, renaming the spirits with Roman names. Water remained important - be it stream, pool or well - and they made offerings and invocations to spirits who dwelt in such places. This follows traditions observed from Mesolithic times such as those at Blick Mead. A Roman lead curse has been found there. Curses found in Britain tend to be nasty, seeking vengeance from the gods for some misdemeanour. Wherever such are discovered, investigation shows such curses are usually found on sites where the Romans had built temples - suggesting they were building on an established ancient tradition, where there was an existing awareness of the power of place, where - as the Romans expressed it - a *genius loci,* (local spirit), dwelt.

The Romans built a shrine around the Cuckoo Stone - as they so often adapted older, indigenous shrines it is likely they were perpetuating a tradition on the site. They had a small village nearby and there are the footings of a large rectangular Roman building. Towards the end of the Roman period, two hoards of coins were buried at the Cuckoo Stone. Nearby, a dog skull pierced with four nails was found buried with a young child. It is not the only site to have this type of finding which is evidence of a dog cult in Celtic times. Dogs were associated with healing. 'Cu' is Celtic for dog, perhaps providing the stone with its name. As the Stonehenge landscape encodes so much astronomical information, perhaps the name is a reference to the dog star, Sirius.

The Romans were aware of Stonehenge. Finds of coins, pottery have been found at the stones. They provide evidence of Romans or Romano-British visiting the site. They may even have tried to investigate it for themselves, as some of the finds were deep in the ground. A possible surgical instrument was amongst finds - perhaps they were also using following an old tradition of using it in their own way as a place of healing.

The Saxons

The Saxons arrived in this country at the decline of the Roman empire. The Anglo Saxons had a rich artistic culture, producing epic poems such as *Beowulf* and producing sophisticated metalwork. Locally, an Anglo Saxon disc brooch was found a short distance from Blick Mead, linking it to Anglo Saxon settlements in Amesbury. The church there of St Mary and St Melor has Anglo Saxon beginnings. Three miles west of Stonehenge at the village of Shrewton, a Saxon cemetery has been found.

It may have been their desire to identify with place that gives us the name by which we now know the monument. 'Stan' is Saxon for stones. 'Henge' means 'hanging', generally believed to be referring to the lintels which appear to 'hang' on top of the uprights. Associating themselves with place led them to identify with existing oral traditions, adopting local histories and renaming the heros with their own historical figures. Another interpretation of the name is 'Stanhengist' - Hengist's stones, referring to a Saxon chieftain by the name of Hengist who, according to legend, is supposed to have performed a massacre on the site. This may be merging with an existing older oral tradition which told of a massacre - possibly even a cosmic one occurring at the end of the last Ice Age. When the Saxons came to this country it was a time when cultural identity with place was important. It would have been politically imperative to form an identity and history with a land to which they were strangers.

The name could alternatively be a combination of Saxon and Celtic, as were many names in the west of England. In Cornish, 'hen' is Cornish for 'old', which would give us quite simply a meaning of 'ancient stones'. Additionally, 'hengan' can roughly be translated as 'old stories and dances', a carol - a song sung whilst dancing in a circle, something that may have been done within the stones. An old name for the stones is the 'Giant's Carol' - a 'carol' being a dance performed in a circle with the dancers singing. This may be something that was done at the site in order to invoke energy and the power of whichever spirit they called upon. Dancing may also have been in imitation of the earth going round the sun. Another name was the 'Giant's Dance'. The name gave rise to the later story that the stones were in fact people, turned to stone for doing something dreadful like dancing on the Sabbath Day.

The Saxons may inadvertently have given us the name for the stones we now call sarsens - "sazzans," in the old Wiltshire dialect. On Chotonagpur Plateau in India, there are big stone slabs known as "sasans". The word may have derived from a long-forgotten word in the Indo-European language of the Neolithic western world and Asia, from which the Latin word developed. Latin for rock is saxum, (plural saxi). When the Romans were succeeded by the Saxons, the similarity in the name may have given them an affinity with them, an identity with the place. In Wales, "Saesons" are Saxons.

The Saxons may also give us the origins of the name for the Heel Stone. The Celtic name for the stone is *clach na freos heol*, (the stone of the rising sun), so the Saxons may have combined *Heol* with their *stan* for stone, the 'sun stone', orientating us towards the sun setting at the midwinter solstice and rising at the midsummer sunrise. One of the legends associated with Stonehenge may have developed from its Celtic name:

According to legend, the devil brought the stones to the site in a single night, hoping to confound the generations to come as to just what it was. Unfortunately for him, he was watched by a friar, or priest, who was hiding in a ditch. When the devil caught sight of him, he picked up one of the stones and threw it at the friar, hoping to kill him. The friar saw what was happening, turned and ran, with the result that when the stone landed, it hit him on the heel. As he was such a very holy man, instead of striking him dead, it left the imprint of his heel in the stone. It did the friar no damage at all.

The Heel Stone looks a little like a whale's head and looking towards the 'eye', that is where the friar's heel print can be seen - a natural weathering depression shaped like a footprint. In turn, the story may have combined the Celtic name with another legend which tells that the monument was built by the enchanter

Merlin as a monument to his mother. He left his heel print in one of the stones, (no. 14 of the outer circle), as his signature. This can be likened to the Egyptian architect Imoteph leaving his signature on the earliest pyramids.

There is an Anglo Saxon poem, *The Ruin*, which, if it describes Stonehenge, would be the first English reference to the monument. Since 1865 it has been considered to be about Bath. Equally it could be alluding to an allegorical place. It is included in the Exeter Book, a sort of miscellany dating to 960 - 990 AD but the poem itself is probably a couple of centuries earlier. The translation below is by Dr Graeme Davis and it could easily be referring to Stonehenge and Blick Mead.

The Ruin

Fate has shattered the wondrous, mighty stone. The city is broken, the work of giants has perished. The top parts have fallen, the high rocks tumbled, the beams are bereaved, the mortar has failed, broken holes provide no shelter from the storms; the old ones are eaten away. The worldly craftsmen, now decayed, now departed, are held in the clutch of the earth; they have rested in the grip of the grave while a hundred generations of their nation have passed away. Only the wall, lichen-covered and stained red, has outlived one kingdom after another, and remains standing against the storms, its high curves fallen.
(damaged section of manuscript)
(What the builders') hearts knew, their craft expressed through zeal for circle building. The foundations of the walls were wondrously supported and the surrounding earth-banks shone. There were many (standing stones) with many pinnacles, full of the sounds of war and of much banqueting and of earthly pleasures. Then swift fate changed all that. Men perished everywhere; the day of pestilence came; death took all the host of men; the warriors were stolen. The bulwarks decayed. The site was in ruins because those who should have repaired it were dead. Therefore these structures are mournful and these curved, red-stained remnants have fallen away from the circular beams. In their downfall they sank down to the ground, smashed to

pieces.

Before in this place had been many men, joyous and splendidly adorned with bright gold, proud and drunk, shining in their armour, with treasure, silver, worked gems, wealth, riches, perls and the bright fortress with its wide dominion. Near where the raised stones stand there is a warm stream with a wide spring. A wall surrounds it all, and within its bright circuit were the baths, warm and ready, conveniently placed. The flow … over the grey stone warms streams … the round pool … warm …where the baths were.

Eleventh Century

Queen Elfrida, the first crowned queen of England, (Bath Abbey 973), lived at Amesbury in the tenth century. She had a church built very close to the spring at Blick Mead reputedly in contrition for the murder of her stepson Edward.

About eighty years after Edward's death, the relics of Breton saints were brought to England to escape the hordes invading France at that time. Amongst them were the relics of St. Melor, which tradition says rested on the altar of Amesbury church and to whom the church is dedicated - it is the church of St Mary and St Melor.

Melor had lived in Brittany. He was heir to his father's kingdom but a jealous uncle, who would inherit if Melor was out of the way, tried several ways of disposing of him. He had one of Melor's arms and one of his legs hacked off. The removal of limbs is something that would render an heir totally unsuitable as a king. A king had to lead his people in battle. He could have no physical sign of weakness. The king and the land were one, so a maimed king would bring a maimed land, infertility and plague. However, Melor was given a silver prosthesis which he used almost as if his own had grown again. Eventually the uncle had Melor's head hacked off.

Stories of limbs that grew again were a theme of Celtic myth. They are a way of telling of Nature's continual cycle of death and regrowth and of the phases of the moon. Melor's story is very similar to the story of the Celtic god Nuada silver hand, who regenerated a silver hand. He was the Celtic god of healing, dogs and water - the healing with which the area is connected, the spring at Blick Mead and the river and the tentative connection with the dog cult at the Cuckoo Stone. The shamanic spirits of the Palaeolithic and Neolithic were personified in Celtic myth, which may be why they survived into the Christian era as they were not obvious deities that threatened the new religion. The church at Amesbury may have been dedicated to St Melor because there was an existing, very similar tradition - such as one surrounding Nuada - in order to Christianise the story. This happened in many places where there was a strong oral tradition - a Christian saint with a similar story was adopted in the hopes that the people would forget their pagan hero. However, the adoption of an unusual saint may provide a link with an ancient tradition of healing and nature's cycles of renewal at Blick Mead and Stonehenge. This tradition continued in Medieval times, as people used to bring spring water to the site, pour it over the stones and then wash in it, hoping for a cure for their ailments.

Twelfth Century

The very first writing we can be absolutely certain refers to Stonehenge was by Henry of Huntingdon, who had been asked Bishop Alexander of Lincoln to write a history of England. Referring to Stonehenge in about 1130 AD he wrote:

"Stanenges, where stones of wonderful size have been erected after the manner of doorways, so that doorway appears to have been raised upon doorway, and no-one can conceive how such great stones have been raised aloft, or why they were built there."

The earliest written account of the building of Stonehenge is the legend of Merlin the Enchanter, written down in 1138-9 AD by Geoffrey of Monmouth in his *Historia Regum Britanniae*. Geoffrey always claimed he was writing from older sources. These are largely Welsh texts, primarily the Mabinogion, depicting Arthur as a Dark Age king and his kingdom set in Wales. The stories are typical hero/epic tales, familiar to its listeners, stories handed from parent to child, which later became the inspiration for stories of King Arthur and his Knights of the Round Table. Knowledge could be handed on through generation to generation by story tellers repeating word for word their stories but who didn't need to understand their hidden meaning. Access to the information carried in them was restricted to only a few initiates. By the time they were written down, they were already millennia old.

Invading peoples had, through the ages, adopted the local heroic deeds, claiming them as their own culture, as identity with place was very important and consequently associations with Arthur are spread over the whole of the British Isles, thus suggesting the stories were already old in the era in which Geoffrey of Monmouth set them.

Part of the story that deals with Stonehenge precedes Arthur and could be part of an oral tradition which had its roots at the time when the monument was actually being built, a story passed down the generations by word of mouth. It deals with the bluestone phase of the monument. Some of the archaeological facts coincide remarkably with the legend and it is interesting to match the two together. Even after Geoffrey wrote it down, it was accepted as fact for a further five hundred years.

Geoffrey of Monmouth set his story at the decline of the Roman Empire, around the fourth century AD, which was as far back as people were aware of at the time when he was writing. Essentially, the legend is an oral tradition, told by people who committed their knowledge to memory. Over centuries people have tried to tie the stories to place. It is not possible to tie them even to time. The story may refer to actual historical events or it may refer to cosmological events, complex and convoluted. Many of the Arthurian legends are firmly rooted in Celtic mythology - there is an old Welsh legend where Arthur fights for the daughter of the Sun every May Day until the Day of Judgement. This is a solar legend, telling how nature performs.

The following legend is a version of the one written down by Geoffrey in his *History of Kings*, with the beginning embellished by his *Life of Merlin*.

The Legend

The Devil was angry. He was very angry. For three hundred years he had been angry. He paced the halls of hell in his anger. He bellowed with rage. He was angry because, so we are told, when Jesus was crucified, died and buried, he went down into Hell and gave the Devil and his daemons a very bad time. He told them just how badly they behaved. Worse than that, the people on Earth wanted to be good like Jesus and were no longer so willing to do the bad things the Devil wanted them to do. So the Devil was very, very angry. He plotted and planned to send a man to Earth to be just as bad as Jesus was good. He sent his daemons to Earth to make sure the baby was born. And as soon as he was born, the child Merlin could walk and talk. But the Devil had made a mistake. For Merlin's mother was a very pious lady who prayed continually to God, so although Merlin inherited his father's supernatural powers of prophecy and foresight, he inherited nothing of his nasty nature. He grew from a kind and gentle boy into a good and wise man. Thus when he was just ten years old, he became known as the King's Prophet to a British chieftain called Vortigern.

Vortigern, in a pact with a Saxon named Hengist, had fought a great battle on Salisbury Plain, killing a great many British kings and warriors. Amongst them was the Roman Emperor Constantine. Constantine was meeting with Vortigern and Hengist to draw up a peace treaty but he and his troops were ambushed. His young son Ambrosius was hidden away to be brought up in safety, across the English Channel in Brittany. Vortigern fled then into Wales to build himself a stronghold against his enemies. By day the builders raised Vortigern's Tower but by night their work fell down. So Vortigern consulted his wizards. They told him he should find a boy who never had a father, kill him and sprinkle his blood on the foundations. Then, and only then, would the tower stand.

Vortigern sent his troops out throughout the land trying to find such a boy. At last they came to the town of Caermarthon and as they rested by the gate, they overheard two young boys quarrelling. One of them was heard to say:

"Well, anyway, Merlin - no-one knows who YOUR father is!"

So the soldiers took the young Merlin, with his mother, to Vortigern. When questioned, his mother said it was true, she did not know who Merlin's father was - that as she slept in her nunnery a daemon had visited her and later Merlin had been born. Vortigern then took Merlin up to the tower, intending to kill him. But when they got there, Merlin threw up his arms and started to prophecy. He told Vortigern that under the foundations was a pool where two dragons fought and that was why the tower would not stand. The pool was searched for, found and drained and, sure enough, there were the two dragons. First, up flew a white one - that Merlin said represented Vortigern - then up flew a red one that Merlin said represented Aurelianus Ambrosius. The two dragons fought and the red one killed the white one. In the chaos that followed, Merlin managed to escape.

The very next day, Ambrosius arrived on the shores of Britain, at Totnes in Devon. He brought with him a huge army. He was seeking revenge from Vortigern for the deaths of his father, the Roman Emperor Constantine and his older brother Constans.

They marched off up into Wales, found Vortigern's Tower and burnt it to the ground, with Vortigern and his people still in it. They went on to drive out the pagan Saxons, led by Hengist, who were beginning to invade Britain at this time. This done, Ambrosius drew together all the kingdoms of Britain under his one kingship.

A little later he was riding across Salisbury Plain when he came to a very sacred and spiritual area with over three hundred burial mounds. When he enquired what they were, he was told that here lay the bodies of past kings and warriors of Britain. Ambrosius was much moved by the sight, realising his father was amongst those buried there, and declared that a memorial should be set up, the like of which had never been seen in this country before, to stand forever. While his architects were drawing up designs for such a memorial, he himself stayed at a settlement nearby which afterwards took his name and became known as Ambrosius' town, or Amesbury, as it is now known.

No-one could produce a design that he liked and so eventually he sent for the now famous enchanter Merlin. Merlin came up from his deep, dark mysterious valleys in Wales and advised the king to send for the stone circle known as the Giants' Dance, from Mount Killaraus in Ireland, because the stones were big in size and reputation. They had a mystery and a healing power to cure almost any ailment. Ambrosius liked the sound of that and so he sent his brother Uther with fifteen hundred warriors to steal away the stone circle but when they got there they found they could not move a single stone so much as a hair's breadth. So Merlin went then and put together his own engines and laid the stones down so lightly as none could believe it. He brought them back across water with music and magic to where they stand to this day just outside of Amesbury.

Soon after he had finished erecting the circle, a great comet appeared in the sky, resembling the head of a great fire breathing dragon. Merlin wept, because he knew it foretold the death of his friend Ambrosius. He also prophesised that Ambrosius' brother Uther would become king after him and that he would reign under the sign of the dragon that the comet had resembled. Indeed he became Uther Pendragon, or Uther Dragon-head. Finally, Merlin foretold that Uther's son would become the greatest king of all. And so it was that Merlin's finest achievement began. He saw to it that Uther had this very special son and on the wild, wet and windy night that he was born in the isolated castle at Tintagel, in Cornwall, Merlin carried the baby away to bring him up in a place of safety until it was time to bring to kingship - Arthur, the last of the Romans, first of the Britons; the Once and Future king who ruled in a Golden Age with his legendary knights of the Round Table.

But that is not quite the end of the story, for it is said that Merlin sleeps yet - some say in a hollow hill, some say in a grove of whitethorn trees and some say he is merely hidden in the glory of the air around until such times as Arthur and his country have need of him. And then he will wake again.

Geoffrey's *Historia* was hugely successful, the most popular medieval secular book. It was translated into Norman French by a

Jersey man by the name of Wace, under the title of 'Roman de Brut' (c. 1155).

Thirteenth Century

In 1220, work began building a cathedral ten miles from Stonehenge, for what was to become the city of Salisbury. Popular thought was that the edifice should embody both a model of the cosmos and an image of the perfect world to come. The aesthetics of numbers and proportion were used to provoke a sense of divine presence. Divisions of time were incorporated into the original design of Salisbury Cathedral - it was built with 365 windows, (days in a year), 12 doors, (months in a year), and 8,760 pillars, (hours in a year). This was a renaissance of ideals by Plato, (who lived 2,000 years after Stonehenge was built, 427 - 347 BC), who held that numbers were of paramount importance and without which the cosmos would return to chaos. 500 years prior to Plato, King Solomon, ruling 971 - 931 BC, stated "...but thou hast ordered all things in measure and number and weight." - *Solomon 11.20.* 1,500 years before Solomon, the numbers of stones used in the design of Stonehenge recorded lunar cycles. To fully understand the design of the monument and the knowledge encoded in it, we would need to understand the philosophers of the day - whose thoughts we do not have access to - but whose ideas were passed down the generations.

Fourteenth - Sixteenth Centuries

The first drawing of Stonehenge appears in the Scala Mundi - the *Chronicle of the World* - dating to 1440 AD. It is a tiny bird's eye view drawing showing four trilthons, held together with mortise and tenon joints. It describes how Merlin "not by force, but by art, brought and erected the giant's ring from Ireland."

In late mediaeval times, stories of King Arthur and his Knights of the Round Table became popular all across Europe with their ideals of chivalry. Merlin remained Arthur's shadowy advisor. In England, Arthur was adopted as a hero for political reasons. Sir Thomas Mallory, set his version of the Arthurian Legend, *'Le Morte D'Arthur'*, (published by Caxton in 1485), on Salisbury Plain. In probability he modelled his Guinever on Eleanor of Provence, the wife of King Henry III. In *'Le Morte D'Arthur'*, Arthur's wife Guinever was incarcerated in Amesbury Abbey after her adultery with Sir Launcelot was discovered. Eleanor lived out her days in Amesbury Abbey.

By 1480, a version of Wace's translation included an illustration of Merlin adjusting a lintel on a trilithon, which remains an iconic image.

The antiquary John Leland, (1503 - 1552), wrote a variation of Geoffrey of Monmouth's story whereby the stones were brought from somewhere on Salisbury Plain 'which was both near the site fixed upon, and was also remarkable for the enormous size of its blocks.' This is the first written reference to the location the sarsen stones were brought from.

Seventeenth Century

A brief account of Merlin building Stonehenge appears on John Speed's map of Wiltshire, 1610 AD, almost five hundred years after it was first written down, suggesting it remained the most popular view.

The first known excavations at Stonehenge were by Dr William Harvey and Gilbert North in the early C17th. This may be what triggered the interest of the king, Charles I, (1600 - 1649), in Stonehenge. At that time there were no such things as archaeologists, so it fell to the best architects of the day, who designed modern buildings to try and decipher the mysterious origins of the ancient monument. It was on the instruction of King Charles that his architect and Surveyor of Works, Inigo Jones, (1573 – 1652), investigated Stonehenge in the 1620's. Jones had studied architecture in Italy and brought the Palladian style of architecture, based on geometrically perfect proportions, to this country. He envisaged the monument as originally standing as an oval of six trilithons surrounded by a perfect circle of thirty upright stones, capped by a ring of thirty lintels to form a complete, closed circle. In the centre was a single stone which he marked on his plan as the Altar Stone. He came to the conclusion that it had been built as a Roman temple because of its perfect symmetry - the design he assumed it to have been - that being their style of building. In 1647, his nephew John Wood, suggested that Stonehenge was never actually completed. Wood based his design of the Circus at Bath on Stonehenge. It has thirty houses in place of the sarsen uprights of the outer circle. It represents the Sun on Earth and the nearby Crescent to represent the moon.

Around this time a historian, antiquarian, topographer by the name of William Camden, (1551 - 1623), wrote the first chorographical survey of the British Isles. He named the area surrounding Blick Mead 'Vespasian's Camp,' after a Roman emperor who probably never visited Britain. This corresponds with the view popularised at the time by Inigo Jones that

Stonehenge had been built by the Romans.

The king was not the only person interested in finding out the origins of Stonehenge. According to John Aubrey, (1626 – 1697), writing in the late seventeenth century, one of the trilithons fell as a result of the Duke of Buckingham digging around its foundations earlier that century. The Duke had unknowingly dug into a prehistoric pit, finding but discarding the skulls of cattle and other animals and charcoal, which would be of considerable interest with today's technology. John Aubrey noticed depressions in the ground just inside the henge which, four hundred years later, were termed Aubrey holes after him. They proved to be pits dug shortly after the henge itself. Aubrey considered the monument had been built before the Romans arrived in this country and attributed it to the Druids. He also referred to the central and focal stone as the Altar Stone.

Another architect who was inspired by Stonehenge is Sir Christopher Wren, (1632 - 1723). The son of a vicar, he was brought up in the nearby village of East Knoyle. In the fashion of the time, he carved his name on one of the upright stones. When he designed St. Paul's Cathedral in London, the dimensions of the dome were based on the outer circle of sarsens stones at Stonehenge.

Eighteenth Century

During the following century, Stonehenge and its immediate landscape were investigated by an amateur archaeologist by the name of William Stukely, (1687 – 1765). He left us a hugely valuable resource in the form of accurate drawings of monuments and landscape as they were when he saw them. He was influenced by Aubrey's work, again attributing it to the Druids. He surveyed Stonehenge, Avebury and many other ancient monuments, producing accurate drawings of them. It was Stukely who noticed the Cursus, by then grassed over and silted up and therefore so much less obvious as a monument in the landscape. He suggested it had been built by the Romans for chariot racing, which he envisaged them watching whilst picnicking amongst the stones. He subsequently named it the Cursus, from the Latin for course. In 1740 he published *Stonehenge, A Temple Restor'd to the British Druids*. In so doing, he focused on their ideas, rather than their rituals and saw them as practising an ancient proto-Christian religion.

He believed that the Ancients expressed Truth by symbols and hidden images. Speaking the name of a god could unleash untold power into the world. He offered considerable evidence that in ancient times the ultimate deity, the supreme fountain of all being, was symbolised by a circle, across the world from China to America. Just as the Christian Trinity, this deity could be expressed as threefold. The second symbol found throughout the ancient world was a snake - the divine emanation from the circle. The third symbol was wings on the circle - the spirit, the *anima mundi*.

Stukely believed the patterns of stone circles were symbols of the ultimate deity. From studying Stonehenge and Avebury, twenty miles north, he noticed that across the world, ancient temples appeared to built as gigantic patterns of these symbols. A simple circle which, having no beginning or end, was a symbol of infinity, a symbol of God. Some circles had processional ways, avenues, emanating from them. Stonehenge has an avenue snaking away towards the river. Avebury had an avenue snaking from each of its massive circles. Stukely interpreted these avenues as representative of snakes. He claimed these serpentine temples were called 'Dracontium' in ancient times.

In legend, temples were often kept by dragons or serpents. In the ancient world serpents were 'wonderful motion without legs,' thought to be like that of the gods. 'Gods having snakes' feet' meant that their motion was smooth and sweeping without the alternate use of legs. The bisid tongue was the symbol of eloquence - the ancients thought snakes brought forth their young from their mouths, as are words. Their enchanting power was real. In Egypt, snakes of a golden colour reflected back the beams of the sun. The snake's habit of throwing off its skin - and old age with the skin - symbolised a return to youth, a strong symbol of resurrection and immortality.

Later people became idolatrous and a serpent placed in a box was worshipped for itself, rather than what it symbolised. According to Greek mythology, serpents licked the ears of Helenus and Cassandra to sharpen their hearing so they could hear the council of the gods, thereby becoming great prophets. Stukely interpreted this to mean that a standing stone or serpentine temple was somewhere to hear the words of gods - which coincides with the concept that people had communicated with their ancestors there from the time when the Aubrey holes were first dug.

This was the basis under which Stukely formed a new order of Druids, in his eyes emulating the Iron Age Druids whom he supposed had erected the monument. The association of Druids and Stonehenge remains fixed in people's imaginations.

The first person to investigate the barrows was William Cunnington, (1754 – 1810) - also an amateur archaeologist of the eighteenth century. Due to ill-health, he had been advised to spend time outside, which he duly did, riding across Salisbury Plain on horseback. He soon became fascinated by the small round hills which cluttered the landscape and he decided to dig into them to find out what they were. He later joined forces with Sir Richard Colt Hoare and their discoveries were carefully documented and published in 1812, two years after Cunnington's demise. This was Colt Hoare's first volume of *Ancient Wiltshire*, containing plans of how the monument actually looked, not how he thought it may have looked like when first built.

It became known that the barrows contained skeletons. Skeletons were a desirable commodity to doctors in the nineteenth century who were interested in anatomy. One of these was the superintendent of Devizes asylum, Dr. Thurman, a native of Yorkshire. He was more interested in studying the bones for his work than in the monuments. He later published a scholarly study of his findings. It could be said that these early archaeologists dug into the barrows with more enthusiasm than expertise. The only barrows that have not been investigated are the King barrows, on the high ridge of land east of Stonehenge.

It was during the C18th that people learnt how to break the hard sarsen stone. First a fire needs to be lit under them and then cold water poured on them so that they split horizontally or vertically when hit with a hammer. There was still the considerable effort of carting them way. Although a single monolith broken into bricks would be enough to build a small cottage, breaking up the sarsens was really more trouble than they were worth. Even so, blocks of sarsen appear in buildings locally and which may have originated from Stonehenge.

A large proportion of the bluestones are now missing. The stone is much softer than sarsen stone - so much so that people used to stop at the town of Amesbury, two miles away, go to the blacksmiths' shop and hire a hammer and then go to Stonehenge and chip away little pieces of bluestone to take away as souvenirs. Not only were these mementoes but the stone was said to have a healing property.

Nineteenth Century

In the July of 1820, Constable, (1776 - 1837), visited Stonehenge and made a sketch which became the base for a large watercolour displayed at his last exhibition in 1836 at the Royal Academy. It was captioned:
"The mysterious monument... standing on a bare and boundless heath, as much unconnected with the events of the past as it is with the uses of the present, carries you back beyond all historical records into the obscurity of a totally unknown period."

It has been suggested that Constable saw himself as a ruin after the death of his wife - art not only depicts its subject but also how the artist responds to it, what is mirrored back to him. Stonehenge had become of particular interest to artists in a time when there was a growing appreciation for desolate landscapes and ancient ruins. Constable's contemporary, Joseph Mallord William Turner, (1775 - 1851), made many sketches of Stonehenge during his lifetime.

The advent of the railways meant people could visit sites such as Stonehenge for themselves. Increased interest resulted in books and articles for journals on the subject. One theory that surfaced was that the ruined condition of Stonehenge was due to the biblical Great Flood.

In Victorian times, Stonehenge was used for a variety of entertainments such as excursions, hare coursing, falconry, musical concerts and even cricket. The Stonehenge cricket ground was used between 1830 - 1920 but was not actually among the stones using the trilithons as gigantic wickets, as depicted by an old cartoon which shows Old Father Time bowling out the Druids.

Barrow digging had become a popular pastime for landed gentry. In 1839, a naval officer by the name of Captain Beamish dug as indiscriminately as the Duke of Buckingham had done a couple of centuries earlier, this time digging north east of the Altar stone and thereby obliterating the opportunity for discoveries of significance in the centre of the stones.

The Egyptologist Sir Flinders Petrie, 1853 - 1942, surveyed Stonehenge in 1874. He thought the same as John Wood, that the outer circle of sarsen stones had never been completed. Petrie invented a system of numbering the stones, in order to identify them individually. This was published in his *Stonehenge: Plans, Descriptions and Theories*. Previously, superstition told that it was supposed to be impossible to count the stones twice and arrive at the same total. The first written reference to this was by the poet, Sir Philip Sidney, writing in 1598. King Charles II had spent time trying to count them while his friends were making plans for his escape from the country, in 1651. The famous English author of the nineteenth century, Charles Dickens, mentioned the story but added bad luck to attempting to count them. This was probably in deference to the superstition that the devil would gain power over anyone trying to count something of a supernatural nature. Merlin, the legendary builder, was after all reputedly the devil's son. The writer Daniel Defoe wrote of a baker who tried to place a loaf on each stone in order to count them - similar tales are told of other sites.

One of the portal stones that had stood at the main entrance between the Heel Stone and the circle of stones was by this time lying down flat in the henge bank. It had iron ore stains on it which looked like blood, especially in wet weather. People thought it had been used for sacrificial slaughter and subsequently called it the Slaughter stone. There are two stone holes to the west of it which, assuming it is lying over its own stone hole, implies there were originally three portal stones. By this time, many of the stones had fallen or were leaning precariously. Letters appeared in the local press and were sent to the Times complaining about the state of disrepair. Pressure was exerted on the landowner to fence it in. Scaffolding was erected to support some of the stones, which resulted in the public demanding that the whole site should be restored. The general feeling was that a monument of such importance should not be the personal property of a single landowner.

Despite this turmoil, at the turn of the century although tourism to Stonehenge was increasing, the land around was still being used as pasture land, the traditional land usage. The shepherd watching over his flock by night looked up and watched the stars; the constellations continuing their eternal course, much as pastoralists had done for thousands of years.

Twentieth Century

On the last night of the nineteenth century, a storm howled over Salisbury Plain. The skies of history hurtled over the storm clad Stonehenge, heralding the approach of the infant twentieth century. The Earth shuddered. Was it her vision of entering a century shortly to be beset by two world wars? Was it a warning against human nature? Was it the old belief - a doom laden prophecy that the fall of a stone precipitated the monarch's death? Certainly within 13 months, Queen Victoria was dead. For the storm had dislodged a lintel stone at Stonehenge. It is said that the reverberations were felt two miles away in Amesbury.

How did the new landowner, Sir Edmund Antrobus feel? When concern was expressed to his late father on the safety of the stones, largely in the years following the Ancient Monument Protection Act 1882, he denied there to be 'danger of any sort,' although when challenged he wrote "I fully recognise the debt I owe to the Public, as holder of a Monument of such interest..." Early in the new century, Sir Edmund took advice. As a result, the largest stone on the site, the huge leaning stone of the central trilithon, was restored to its proper position under the direction of Professor Gowland. The Heel Stone also received this attention and other stones propped by wooden supports. A fence was erected around the stones and a charge made of one shilling entrance fee, in order to pay a policeman to prevent people damaging the stones.

Promptly a public outcry ensued and a long and expensive law suit against Sir Edmund Antrobus followed by way of protest. The judge, Mr Justice Farwell, ruled in favour of the defendant as owner of the site against representatives of the British Public. However, the fence remained open on the Eastern side where there was a well-worn right of way.

Around the same time, Sir Norman Lockyer attempted to date the monument by very precise astronomical observations of the midsummer solstice sunrise. The direction of this was traditionally recognised as the axis of the monument and had changed since it was built due to the shift in the Earth's axis. Unfortunately it would seem his thorough calculations were based on unsound information.

In 1903 Sir Edmund decided to offer to sell Stonehenge and 1,300 acres of land to the army, who for the previous seven years had been buying up land on Salisbury Plain to establish a training area. He asked £125,000. 'Beyond the means of the country' was the curt response. Less than a decade later the first military airfield in the country would be built very close to Stonehenge, when the army wanted the stones taken down to facilitate the taking off and landing of aircraft. They had missed their opportunity. When the army turned him down, Sir Edmund then dropped the price to £50,000 from 'some public body', (who were constantly telling him what to do with the site anyway), for 'Stonehenge, including an area surrounding it not exceeding eight acres.'

When Antrobus died in 1915, he had no heir to inherit - his son having been killed early in the First World War. His property went up for auction on 25th September, 1915. Many locals attended, hoping to buy businesses and homes they already occupied as tenants. Little interest was taken in lot no. 15 - Stonehenge and 30.730 acres of downland. Who would want a bit of grazing land with a big pile of stones in the middle? Who would want the expense of maintaining them so the public could clamber all over them, trampling across the land to get there? A decent farm with almost 100,000 acres of land had just sold for £5,600.

The auctioneer, Sir Howard Frank, was aware that it was considered by some to be one of the wonders of the ancient world. He had told journalists that as an auctioneer he would not insult himself by attempting to describe Stonehenge, 'when the Royal Archaeological Society have been kind enough to give us their own description. We are content to leave the details to those who are competent to speak about it.' He suggested a starting figure of £5,000. No response. He cajoled his audience and eventually a gentleman raised his hand. The bidding dragged on between two bidders but eventually the hammer dropped at £6,600. Sir Howard announced that 'Stonehenge has been bought by Mr C.H.E. Chubb of Bemerton Lodge, Salisbury.' Most of those who then cheered did so because Stonehenge had been bought by a local man. Chubb was a barrister, who had once taught at Bishop Wordsworth's school, Salisbury. He was very insistent that the decision to buy Stonehenge was not his alone but a joint one between himself and his wife. They wished to assure the public that the monument would continue to be preserved and protected by fencing and a custodian appointed. Asked about his plans for the future of it, he said he hadn't had time to think about it.

"You see, I hadn't the slightest idea that I was going to buy Stonehenge when I entered the saleroom. But while I was in the room I thought a Salisbury man ought to buy it and that was how it was done."

Three years later on 26th October 1918, he and his wife were to gift Stonehenge to the Commissioners of Works for the benefit of the nation. This was done with much speechifying in the centre of Stonehenge. The Deed of Gift bequeathing Stonehenge sets out a set of conditions, the first of which 'that the public shall have free access to the premises hereby conveyed and every part thereof on payment of such reasonable sum per head not exceeding one shilling for each visit and subject to such conditions as the Commissioners of Works in the exercise and execution of their statutory powers and duties may from time to time impose.' Later the donors were honoured with a knighthood, becoming Sir Cecil, first baron of Stonehenge, and Lady Chubb.

The government realised they would have to embark on a programme of excavation and restoration. Consequently this was begun in the 1920's under the leadership of Colonel Hawley.

During the dig of 1923-4, Hawley discovered two rings of pits outside of the sarsen circle. At the time it was felt they had been dug to hold a further rearrangement of the bluestones. They are referred to as the Y & Z holes.

In 1925 an aerial photograph was taken a couple of miles away from the monument. It was investigated by Maud Cunnington and proved to be a pattern of concentric pits which had once held timber posts. Because of the likeness in design to Stonehenge, the site was named Woodhenge in contrast and since then a henge has come to be the archaeological term for bank and ditch enclosures, generally a bank and ditch which encloses an area of land used for ritual purposes. These type of monuments are unique to this country. Stonehenge is a stone building inside a henge monument. The lintel stones which 'hang' on top of the uprights determine its classification as a building rather than a stone circle. The ditch at Stonehenge is, unusually, outside the bank and despite giving its name to subsequent henges, Stonehenge is therefore not a true henge in the archaeological sense.

Meanwhile, Colonel Hawley was investigating the Aubrey Holes at Stonehenge. He wrote in his notebooks that the pits had held stones. At the time his colleagues, in particular Maud Cunnington, declared it to be contemporary with Woodhenge and was therefore a timber circle.

Colonel Hawley unearthed finds, such as pieces of cremated bone, too small to be analysed at the time. He reburied some in three trenches known as 'Hawley's graves'. He also kept some cremated bones in a box in his attic but realised they could be discarded if anything happened to him. When Newley was investigating the Mesolithic post holes ten years later, Hawley returned to bury them in the second largest Aubrey Hole.

The programme of excavation and restoration was interrupted by the second world war. In 1947, the first ever trench to be dug across the Cursus was cut by J F S Stone, (1891? – 1957). He was well known for his work in and around Wiltshire, especially at Stonehenge and the Woodhenge area. In 1950, the Society of Antiquaries commissioned an excavation at Stonehenge itself. Dr Stone joined R J C Atkinson, (1920 - 1994), and Stuart Piggott, (1920 - 1996), to undertake the work. They recovered many cremations and developed the phasing that still dominates much of what is written about Stonehenge. The newly developed technique of radio carbon dating was utilized by its developer Willard Libby, an American chemist and Nobel Prize winner. Using one piece of charcoal from a pit, the monument was dated to approximately 2,000 - 1,500 BC, dates which have since been refined. Atkinson noticed the axe head and dagger carvings whilst photographing more modern graffiti. They have an element of Arthurian legend, swords in the stone. He found holes which he dubbed Q & R holes - the pits that had held bluestones when removed from the Aubrey Holes and arranged in the centre as a double horseshoe shape. Lying transversely in the centre of the monument, Atkinson felt that the Altar stone was not in its original position - even allowing for the fact that the partner and lintel of the Great Trilithon had landed on top of it. It does not lie either symmetrically or at right angles to the main axis of the monument. He felt it originally stood upright because of the shaping of it and that it was therefore lying over its own stone hole. He suggested that the eventual design was a fusion of earlier traditions, brought together under a unifying kingship, in the very British art of compromise.

Richard Atkinson was a natural media performer who appeared regularly on television. One BBC TV programme in 1954 featured replica bluestones transported by schoolboys on the Salisbury Avon, from which we derive our current understanding of how they could have been brought from the Preseli mountains to Stonehenge. In his book *Stonehenge,* he writes:

"For who is to say that for the ultimate understanding of Stonehenge, not in terms of the categories of archaeological research but as part of our human inheritance and to that degree as part of ourselves, the aesthetic experience must play a lesser part than the precise and academic dissection of the evidence we recover from its soil?"

In 1955 Alexander Thom, (1894 - 1985), published his theory concerning unit of length common to Neolithic sites which he called the megalithic yard. Overly simplified, the megalithic yard is derived from the length of string needed for a pendulum to pulse a specified number of times for the duration of TIME it takes for a star to move between two set points. This is beautifully illustrated in 'The Royal Art of Astronomy' by R. Eisler as a shepherd sighting the pole star. He holds a staff in one hand and in the other holds up a weighted plumb line against the pole star. A second drawing shows him observing the transit through the meridian of the stars forming the easily recognisable

W of Cassiopeia. Again he has a staff in one hand and has a plumb line held up against the stars. The illustrations are distinctly reminiscent of the hermit card in a deck of tarot cards. Here the hermit holds a staff in one hand and holds a lantern containing a star in the other. Before clocks and calendars, time was measured in seasonal observations and it can be conjectured that whatever its original inception, Stonehenge has been used as such. The movements of the sun and moon across the heavens created a measure for Time itself. Stonehenge thereby created an axis for the world to revolve on and a channel for time to flow into. The dimensions of Stonehenge are, in that sense, measured in Time.

Solstice celebrations were observed throughout the excavations. In 1961, eight wheelbarrows were filled with the broken bottles that littered the site. The following year temporary barbed wire fences were erected as a crowd control measure. During the 1960's it became fashionable to paint graffiti on the stones, especially political comments such as 'Ban the Bomb'.

In 1965, the Beatles filmed 'Help' on Salisbury Plain, with footage of Stonehenge. They stayed at the Antrobus Arms in Amesbury, where hundreds of fans waited outside hoping for a glimpse of their idols. The Rolling Stones also visited the Stones in 1967.

The number of day visitors was increasing and in 1968, facilities were built across the road from the monument. Access was through a tunnel under the road.

Working for English Heritage, Geoff Wainwright led many excavations in England and Wales including Stonehenge, Durrington Walls and Woodhenge. His work at Durrington Walls took place over just three months in the summer of 1967, ahead of building a new road between Amesbury and Durrington. He discovered the Southern and Northern Circles. When he left English Heritage in 1999, Professor Wainwright set up a field project in North Pembrokeshire together with Professor Tim Darvill, (University of Bournemouth), to investigate what the significance of the bluestones was that justified them being brought from the Preseli mountains in Pembrokeshire to set up at Stonehenge.

In 1980 a newly formed group called Wessex Archaeology was set up, based in Salisbury. From there, Julian Richards led the *Stonehenge Environs Project*, which was a detailed study not only of Stonehenge but also the monuments in its surrounding landscape. He contributed parts to programmes about Stonehenge and went on to become a member of the television programme *Time Team*. He is the author of the official English Heritage guidebook on Stonehenge.

In 1974, the pirate radio station Radio Caroline promoted a gathering of people to a festival of Love and Awareness. It was the beginnings of the Stonehenge Free Festival. 'Radio Caroline' was daubed on the stones. The cleaning process damaged the lichens that grow on the stones - but on one, which bore the 'D' and the 'I', yellow lichen grows where the letters had been. Numbers attending the festival had increased to 65,000 by 1984. It was not only the numbers that had increased. Damage to the archaeological sites - such as using the barrows as bread ovens - drug dealing and tension between authorities and festival goers resulted in an attempt to prevent people reaching the site the following year. A four mile exclusion zone was put in place, and approximately 1,300 police drafted in from across the country in order or enforce it. On 1st June 1985, a convey of around six hundred New Age Travellers who had stayed the night before in the Savernake Forest, set off towards Stonehenge. They reached a road block, where police started smashing windows of vehicles and making arrests. People broke through a hedge into a bean field to try and escape. A violent confrontation ensued, subsequently named the Battle of the Beanfield, the police using over zealous tactics against the convoy. The police claimed the travellers had thrown petrol bombs and sticks, the accusation of serious violence against the police was strongly refuted. According to The Observer newspaper, pregnant women and women holding babies were hit by police with truncheons and the police were hitting 'anybody they could reach.' When some of the travellers tried to escape by driving away through the fields, the Observer stated that the police threw truncheons, shields, fire-extinguishers and stones at them in an attempt to stop them. Several travellers had serious head injuries, one had a fractured skull. Dozens more were injured. The Observer and the Independent reported that traveller's vehicles were smashed and set on fire. Over 500 travellers were arrested.

It was not until 2,000 that access was permitted at the stones again, as a result of many years of negotiations with various interested factions.

Twenty First Century

Early in the twenty first century, plans began for a huge archaeological project that began in 2004, the *Riverside Project,* led by Mike Parker Pearson. It furthered the work done by Geoff Wainwright in the 1960's at Durrington Walls. Digging continued until 2011. Analysis of the project finds continues together with finding the exact location where each of the bluestones originated from in the Preseli mountains.

In the autumn of 2008, a team of archaeologists including Julian Richards, Mike Parker Pearson amongst other giants in the field of archaeology obtained a licence to dig for Hawley's finds. Within the previous ten years, technology had advanced sufficiently to obtain dates from small pieces of bone and to tell whether their owner was male or female. They lifted the iron plate Hawley had placed above them and raised the tiny pieces of cremated bones. Digging further to the base of the pit, they concluded that the evidence pointed to the pits having held stone, rather than wood. Ahead of schedule, they dug a little further towards the centre and discovered a cremation that had originally been placed in a leather bag or a birch bark box. The curve of the container could be seen clearly in the ground. Around 60 cremations have been found in the Aubrey Holes but if burials had been placed close to the stones or continued to be placed after the stones were removed, this number would be significantly greater. Investigation showed that some of the remains were already 300 years old when they were buried at Stonehenge. Looking back, we interpret this as ancestor worship, something that persists to this day in such philosophy as the Catholic communion of saints. To Neolithic people who may have had an ongoing relationship with their forebears, care of the ancestors so that they would care for them was just part of the circle of life.

Ahead of opening the new visitors' centre in 2013, a project which included the use of geophysics and lidar photography was undertaken. Although it revealed details such as carvings on the stones and the direction of the dressing which led the eye towards the midwinter solstice sunset, it did not solve the mystery of whether Stonehenge was ever actually completed. It indicated that four stones may have absent from the southern side of the circle, showing that the design never was a perfect circle around a horseshoe. However, parch marks noticed in the dry weather of 2013 showed that the holes were dug for the stones but it will need further investigation to prove whether or not they ever held stones.

Between 2010 and 2014 the Hidden Landscapes project was a collaboration between the University of Birmingham and the Ludwig Boltzmann Institute for Archaeological Prospection and Virtual Archaeology. They used cutting edge technology, such as motorised survey devices, terrestrial lazar scanning, magnetometer surveying, ground penetrating radar, which revealed further insight into the activity around the Stonehenge landscape. It revealed monuments ploughed out in centuries past hitherto unknown. Some of the barrows are multi-phase, complex hengeforms, adding features such as banks and ditches at various times, suggesting a ritual function. It has shown three henge monuments each, probably significantly, with 24 pits roughly one and a half metres wide and one and a half metre deep - a similar size to the bluestone pits. They could therefore have held a stone setting.

This was the project that showed early Neolithic architecture south of the eastern end of the Cursus in the form of a structure with a horned façade, which had not been known in the Stonehenge landscape before. A similar one is known at Skendleby in Lincolnshire, which had a façade of huge split timbers set in a crescent, reminiscent of long barrows which have stone facades. In an area such as the Stonehenge landscape which has no local stone, this would seem a highly feasible alternative. The posts may have been decorated by painting or with carvings.

This technology also revealed that a, (possible), arc of sixty stones had, at a date currently unknown, been erected to the south of the dwellings at Durrington Walls. They lie recumbent up to 70 cm beneath the soil.

The project at Blick Mead, led by David Jacques, has been

ongoing since 2005. Only a small area has been excavated and there is much to be revealed.

There is much to be discovered within the vast Stonehenge landscape and much to be interpreted by future generations. The increase in archaeological technology reaps a harvest of more questions.

Passing on Knowledge

We communicate knowledge to others today through the internet, television and books. What form will communication take in the future? Will our descendants understand us?

The builders of Stonehenge had oral traditions handed down the generations. They had a deep knowledge of astronomy which encoded in the design of the monument. Three and a half thousand years after Stonehenge was built, Geoffrey of Monmouth wrote down the legend of Merlin building Stonehenge. He claimed he was writing down an oral story. He may well have repeated a story with vestiges whose origins and true meaning had long since been forgotten. He set it at the decline of the Roman Empire but when were its origins? According to the legend, Stonehenge was built as a monument to the British kings and warriors who were killed after a great battle - this thread may be euhemerized as the remains of a very early solar legend, referring to the end of the Ice Age, the great Deluge, 10,500 BC when the Earth was massacred by the Heavens.

All across the world myths, national epics, are told which contain such similar events - albeit giving their 'heroes' different names - that it would seem they are all communicating the same knowledge and metaphorical truths. Mythology is a way of passing information down the generations. Within the myths of Greece and Rome, the Kalevah of Finland, the Nihon Shoki of Japan, the Shahrama of Iran, the Nordic Gylfaginning, the Mahabarata of India - to name but a few - are stories that personify the constellations and the movements of sun, moon and planets - vestiges of the same knowledge. The one thing all these scattered countries had in common was the panoply of the heavens above and how the constellations, planets and their movements related to one another. The constellations provided the setting for the hero. For example, in Roman mythology Vulcan, (Greek equivalent - Hephaistos), finds his wife Venus, (Greek equivalent - Aphrodite), with Mars, (Greek equivalent - Ares). He traps them in a net. This could be describing a conjunction of Mars and Venus in the Pleiades. In Arthurian legend, King Arthur discovers he has been cuckolded by his best friend Sir Launcelot with Queen Guinever.

Portable Information

In addition to oral tradition, throughout the stone ages people had conveyed information to one another in the form of cave art. Eventually there came a time when portable art developed - such as the chalk plaques found near Stonehenge. They may convey neuropsychological experience, they may depict the trilithons of Stonehenge but especially in a landscape without cave walls to daub, whatever they convey, they may have been a way of communicating knowledge diagrammatically and pictorially. Pictorial depictions developed in a more familiar and recognisable way in Sumeria, Babylon and Egypt, in the form of hieroglyphics. Thus the first system of written communication evolved, recording information as well as passing it through the generations orally. Pictures continued to be used to express ideas and information and portable art may have been a particularly successful system of recording astronomical events and their effects, alongside stories - in essence, a picture book. It was necessary to record and share these stories, which we now refer to as mythology, because they were significant to the survival of the human species, understood by a few initiates but whose stories could be told and retold in a way that appealed to everyone. In the telling and retelling, they inevitably became diluted over the centuries, their original roots forgotten, their hidden symbols disregarded.

Some people believe that the oldest book mankind has is the legendary book of Hermes Trismegistus - who was the source of all ancient wisdom and knowledge, master of magic, arts and sciences. He is believed to have lived around the C5th BC and to have been contemporary with Moses and the teacher of Plato. The book supposedly contained ancient, esoteric knowledge, encapsulating in diagrams and pictures something very important, perhaps the exactly same knowledge of astronomy observed at Stonehenge. The book of Hermes Trimegistus is considered by some to be the pack of Tarot cards. Apart from the fortune telling devise it became a couple of millennia after Hermes Trimegistus lived, the cards can be used to tell stories and histories. One of these is the history of the Romany people with whom the Tarot deck is so intrinsically linked. Whatever the starting point for them, they certainly travelled through ancient civilizations - like our Neolithic ancestors - and, without reading or writing, perhaps unwittingly took with them a knowledge preceding the ability to encapsulate ideas in glyphs, or to communicate with writing and retained something of ancient knowledge in oral form, together with the pictures and symbols within the Tarot. The cards may originally have been a technical language between people who speculated on the system of the cosmos, incorporating the archetypal heros of mythology. There is an oral tradition which can be told using a deck of Tarot cards which tells of the divisions in time made by the seasons, day and night perhaps mimicking the use of the very first 'picture books'.

"Consider the beginning of the world when, after the Flood, the three sons of Noah ruled in the East. From the stems of Ham, Shem and Japheth sprang our race. First came the worshippers of the sun, the firstborn sons of men, who were shepherds wandering from place to place in search of food. Then came the labourers in the fields, who turned their faces to the star-studded sky at night and became the calculators of Time, and astronomers. And third in order came those who adored the triple-headed witch goddess of the moon. She taught them to dig down into the bowels of the earth and become smiths and metalworkers, and as a further boon she gave them power to cure those stricken down by fevers and sickness. These three branches of the human race united the sum total of their intelligences and discovered the origin of man in the Zodiac which they called Tantara or Tarot. And the four bands of the solstices and of the equinoxes were the four principal heavenly messengers, the four great arms of the luminous cross of the sky, which the sun carries eternally on his back around the earth. The four seasons were the four great books of Brahma and of Hermes Trismegistus, the Magician, the four great voices or oracles of God, the four great angels and messengers, the four great Prophets and Evangelists. The twelve months, by sets of three, were the twelve lesser works of God, the twelve oxen or bulls of the night and day, the twelve tablets of the Law of Moses and of Romulus, wherein are written the Ten Commandments of Manu, God of Buddha, and of Manoel, God of David; the Twelve Sons of Jacob and the twelve Apostles.

"When the Wise Men of the three races, with the aid of Ramu the sun and Chandra the moon, were assured of the justness of their observations, they created the science of astronomy and prepared its rules, which they engraved upon a tablet of stone. And when the circle was traced and the Tantara or Zodiac was composed, the ages of the world began to revolve. The religions of all nations in the world sprang from the primitive worship of Nature - night, day, the moon, the sun, fire, air, water.

"Our Book of the Tarots has three mystical numbers which guide us in its interpretation - the numbers three, four and seven - and there are four colours which are the four aspects of the seasons. And each colour has twice seven cards, which corresponds to the days and nights of the week. There are nine cards and one ace of each suit. These nine cards and nine of each colour signify the nine months of gestation both astral and human. Also the nine cards and one ace of each colour make the thirty six decades of the year. And so from the Tarot pack we may derive the whole plan of the universe!"

This demonstrates something of the essence of cosmic myths, updated as people move through different cultures and civilizations. It is certainly explaining things that are traditionally associated with Stonehenge therefore be interpreted as encapsulating similar knowledge to that encoded within the design of the monument.

Sun Halo over the Stones

PART FOUR

Experiencing Stonehenge

Why Here?

Experience of the warm spring at Blick Mead led to ritual deposition of objects. It was a special place and the people of the Mesolithic knew it. They were in tune with their surroundings, they did not walk on concrete or tarmac as we do but were in direct contact with the surface of the Earth and were aware of things we have long lost the knowledge of. As Louis Slesin says:
"We're electrical beings living in a magnetic environment. Because we're finely tuned to subtle energy fields, when they vary, as they would on top of a mountain, we change biologically and psychologically too."
Stonehenge is built on a seemingly inauspicious site, certainly not on the highest land around and the monument itself is built on the slope, rather than the crest, of the hill. However, the monument has enormous presence, a power of place. We can no longer wander amongst the stones and touch them to absorb something of their potency. But we even though we cannot touch them we can certainly feel them, interact with them, experience them for ourselves. There is something about them that resonates deeply with us - maybe it is some deep ancestral memory, that we are all the descendants of the Stonehenge builders. Maybe it goes back further, before the stones were set in place, where we feel what the people of the Neolithic felt - the subtle energies of the Earth - and respond. Explanations are inadequate, they obstruct direct experience. The experience of a thin place feels special.

The Roman term for spirit of place was genius loci. Later the energy felt at these places was expressed as the presence of a small supernatural being, (puck, fairy, elf, and the like), or mythological animal, such as a dragon. Many such places had stone circles, standing stones or ancient mounds built there.

One explanation for building Stonehenge where they did - in addition to the midwinter solstice sunset/midsummer solstice sunrise alignment indicated by the periglacial stripes - is that it has a power of place, that it is a 'thin' place. There is a powerful and discernable vortex of energy which flows out of the centre of the stones and out across the land, an energy present from before the henge was built which would remain even if the stones should fall.

Think of the Earth as being a living entity, with its life-force carried around its surface in lines, much as our life-force - our blood - is carried around our bodies in our veins. Stonehenge has a concentration of this energy in its centre which flows out between the gaps in the stones like blood pumped out from the heart. Mesolithic and later Neolithic man may have been very aware of this energy, as indigenous people around the world are to this day. The Australian aborigines call these lines song lines. The North American Indians call them the 'Rainbow Serpent'. In the Far East such lines are known as dragon lines. In Egypt and Mexico, the 'feathered serpent' was held in reverence as a symbol of astronomy. *Draco* is Latin for dragon and serpent - the two are interchangeable. In England this energy is now most popularly called Earth energy or ley lines. It was Alfred Watkins who introduced the latter name in 1921, from the old English word lea, for field. He noticed old straight tracks, ley lines, and thought they were prehistoric trading routes based on straight lines between a variety of sighting points. He never attributed any supernatural significance to ley lines, believing them to simply be pathways that had been used for trade or ceremonial purposes, ancient in origin, possibly dating back to the Neolithic.

Many of us are unfamiliar with acknowledging the experience of feeling the atmosphere of place. However, we recognise that people tend to feel better at the coast, that the air is different, the salt is beneficial to aches and pains, the sound of the sea calming. This is biological response to place. At Stonehenge the response is often that it feels calm, peaceful, still, grounded, energised. The energy comes from the planet we live on. It can calm us by flowing into our chakras, our energy centres, so they work to maximum effect. This supports the physical body and provides an optimum environment for healing. Neither it nor the stones can magically take pain or illness away but the power of the place is such that, with awareness and acknowledgement, it can provide the optimum environment for our bodies to work to best effect.

We live in a very visual society so, even if we cannot

immediately feel earth energy, we can see the effect of energy lines by dowsing for them with metal rods, wooden rods or a pendulum, in the same way as it is possible to dowse for water. Dowsing around the stone circle at Stonehenge, the rods or pendulum can indicate energy lines flowing between the stones. In the very centre of the monument, by the altar stone, dowsing rods indicate the 'eye' of a whirlpool of energy, a vortex. There is a theory that the stones were positioned into the ground like great acupuncture needles, to 'tap into' this energy. Energy lines are generally thought of as being healing or strengthening, so this is another connection with healing and renewal at Stonehenge.

A symbol of healing since ancient times is a spiral, often depicted as a snake, coiling around a sword. Energy moves in a spiral even when travelling in a straight line, rather like a spring. There are spiral carvings in ancient rock carvings all over the world, which perhaps symbolises this energy and records something that was important to people living in prehistoric times. Spirals and clockwise motion are associated with stone circles in names such as Giants' Dance, Giant's Carol, suggesting that people danced and walked around the stones. There is also the swirling of earth energy in and out. At Stonehenge it isn't only the horizontal swirling of energy. There's also a vertical one - spiralling skywards and widening and earthwards and widening forming an X shape with Stonehenge the centre. It's an image that is representative of the cosmos - of the elliptical paths of the sun and the zodiacal belt, an image that appears repeatedly in cosmic mythology. It is a neuropsychological image that appears in the human mind. Nature repeating itself and the cosmos imprinted in the human psyche.

The ancients had such an awareness of the cosmos it seems reasonable that they may also have known about the seemingly magical forces that hold the planets in their positions in the universe. There are a number of sites across the world called navels of the Earth. These are sites of particularly strong Earth energy, vortexes - the navel cords attaching the Earth, like a pillar, to the planets, the constellations, the sun. Stonehenge is recognised as a vortex of Earth energy into which energy flows from the cosmos and out, along earth energy lines.

Knowledge of earth energy may have been widespread until late medieval times. The crossing points of ley lines are thought of as being good points to pray on and the altars of many English churches built until 1,000 years ago over older, pagan sites are on such crossing points, as though the builders were aware of something that has now been forgotten. We go to a church not only to pray but also for healing - emotional and spiritual, so yet again there is a connection with healing. However, on the grounds that knowledge is power, it may be that those in authority didn't want ordinary people to know about it and it became associated with witchcraft. The knowledge was hidden in legends about dragons. The legend of Merlin building Stonehenge hints at the 'dragon power' of the leaders Uther and Arthur Pendragon, who reigned under the sign of the dragon. In early times, dragons were forces of good and only later portrayed as evil monsters. A dragon remained on the coat of arms of the monarchs of England until the reign of Elizabeth I, when it was replaced by a unicorn. A century later, William Stukely was writing about Stonehenge in terms of it being a dragon temple.

Earth energy may have been a source of energy that empowered ancient civilisations, for sites of ancient civilisations all over the world are built on the crossing points of significant energy lines - for example the pyramids in Egypt, the Nasca Lines in Peru and the South American temples. Even without understanding it, one can acknowledge the existence of this energy. Some people claim that Earth energy could become the source of a free and inexhaustible supply of power in the future, especially when fossil fuels are exhausted - and that it would therefore be useful to learn more about it and how to tap into it again.

Today

Five thousand years after people started building on the site we now call Stonehenge, people respond to it with passion. It evokes passion as we see reflected in it subjects that particularly interest and inspire us - engineering, astronomy, maths, art, literature, its sheer beauty. People respond to it according to how it makes them feel. It may be a once in a lifetime visit, which has required considerable, effort and expense to achieve. It may be discussion over how it should be managed by the various agencies responsible for its different facets - preserving it for the future whilst allowing access. It may be a sense of ownership - 100 years ago it was still privately owned but since it was given to the nation, it has been claimed by all and that sense of ownership may well go back further, to when our ancestors first built it. It is an icon not just of Britain but of the world, an icon of human endeavour. It remains a mystery to challenge the human imagination. It is seen by many as a sacred monument which continues to be used as a temple.

Stonehenge is unique. There are over 900 stone circles in Britain but Stonehenge is not one of them. It is a building - and as such the first designed architecture in this country. It is unique in having lintels on top of its circle of upright stones, connected with mortise and tenon joints. Tongue and groove joints link the ends of the lintels of the outer circle. Its stones are shaped and dressed. Of the five trilithons originally in the centre, three remain. The west one fell in 1797 and was re-erected in 1958. Of the Great Trilithon, the tallest stone dominates the site whilst its partner and lintel lie across the almost completely submerged Altar Stone. Around the horseshoe, the outer circle is much depleted but the lintels to the north west framing the axis line give an impression of the original appearance. Many of the bluestones are missing or just stubs in the ground, chipped away by visitors in the past. The henge surrounding it is only about two feet high, rather than the original six feet high, time and weather having eroded it. In the right light or weather conditions, the banks of the Avenue can be seen leading north east from the Heel Stone. The main axis of the monument is along the line of the midsummer solstice sunrise and the midwinter solstice sunset.

It was set up five thousand years ago by Neolithic farmers for purposes that we can only guess at. As well as building the monument itself, the builders of Stonehenge also built the beginnings of a modern society because they had to learn to work together and live together. The monument was used for a period of over 1,000 years - between 3,000 and 1,900 BC - when different arrangements of the stones incorporated the ideas and influences of the many different generations of people who brought, built with and rearranged the stones. And when stories of its building were woven into the tapestry of their history, becoming legend. Neolithic farmers used their precious resources in order to build a unique monument, a miracle of prehistoric engineering - a feat which can only be viewed in the imagination. Its reputation is something which grows in the imagination too but at the same time it is inseparable from the physical monument made incomplete by the ravages of time. It is now 4,000 years since the final stage of building was complete. Stonehenge stands on the chalk downland as a testament to its builders, a wonder of the ancient world. Within those silent portals is a mystery to challenge the human imagination, a space for awe and wonder. People were visiting the Stonehenge landscape for at least 5,000 years before the monument was built - and it continues to draw people and to gather mystery and myth around itself like a November mist. Stonehenge is not the story of one people who came, built one edifice and left - but the story of an evolving landscape, an evolving people and an evolving monument.

It is set almost in the centre of Salisbury Plain. This is an area in Southern England which stretches sixteen miles north of Salisbury to the Pewsey Vale and, east to west, from Lugershall to Westbury. North Salisbury Plain has become in the last century the home of the military - their training area encompasses over 100,000 acres. However, without the latter, no doubt much of it would have been built on during the last century, which would have destroyed a very special landscape consisting of 41% of the chalk downland in Britain; the habitat of birds, insects and animals indigenous to this area. Although this makes it one of the least populated parts of the country now, it was not always so. It has become what amounts to a fossilised archaeological landscape with evidence unseen beneath the pasture, of prehistoric settlements - boundaries, fields, flint working sites, small henges, ritual landscaping, Celtic field systems, Iron Age fortresses, Roman occupation and Medieval land use. Due to the fact that much of it lies in a military training area, it is also now largely inaccessible.

To the immediate south of Stonehenge is one of the busiest roads in the country, the A303, following the route of the prehistoric Harrow Way. To its north are open fields grazed by cows and sheep. The Avenue is visible in the right light or weather conditions but the banks are much diminished. The Cursus can only be seen at close proximity or in the distance from the eastern end looking westwards. Some of the barrows have been ploughed out over the centuries but are now protected monuments. Many are visible from the monument, especially on the near horizons. There are small groups of woodland dotted around the landscape. Beyond the horizon to the north east, two miles away as the crow flies, are Durrington Walls and Woodhenge. These monuments covering 6,500 acres, were designated a UNESCO World Heritage Site in 1986, (together with Avebury). The stone circle, the immediate land around it and Woodhenge are in the custodianship of English Heritage. The further surrounding fields are managed by the National Trust, as is Durrington Walls. The Ministry of Defence, the RSPB, farmers and householders are also landowners. Management of the site also falls within the jurisdiction of Natural England, the Highways Agency, Wiltshire Council, Amesbury Town Council, parish councils, DEFRA and the Department for Culture Media and Sport. The site has to be managed with the specific interests of each of these, whilst keeping a balance of protecting it for itself, preserving it for present and future visitors and with providing access at solstices and equinoxes.

Although the stones are roped off to day visitors so we can no longer touch the stones, Stonehenge reaches out and touches us. We are more accustomed these days to respond through the medium of science, through the things we know definitively. We look, we listen but generally are less comfortable with noticing how we feel as a response. We hand over the responsibility of direct experience to the media, to the internet, to what they tell us. We are less accustomed to responding directly, through personal experience. We recognise that the salt air at the coast makes us feel energised but the idea that a place such as Stonehenge may have an effect on us is less familiar. We may not be able to wander amongst the stones or touch them during normal opening hours any longer but we can still allow them to touch us, to feel their energy and the energy of place. It is a 'thin place', a place of energy where this world and the eternal world meld together. In an age when many people seek personal spirituality rather than organised religion, Stonehenge provides a space to experience directly, to notice how we feel, how we respond. It is interesting that at a time when there is a move away from formal religion to a sense of personal spirituality, that people attach their belief system to something older, somewhere our ancestors probably worshipped - although we have no idea what that worship was directed towards or what form their rituals may have taken. We respond to our ancestors, the builders, to something deep within ourselves. Visiting Stonehenge can be an intensely personal and passionate experience. It is a place to feel a connection to the deep past. It is a place to stand in awe and wonder. We continue to respond to and interact with Stonehenge - its appeal crosses time and cultures, whatever the intent of the builders.

Just before the midwinter solstice in 2013, a new visitors' centre was opened to accommodate the increasing number of visitors to Stonehenge. The approach, from any direction, is through farmland. The architecture of the centre includes a 'forest' of squared steel posts and a canopy roof with holes to create a dappling effect on the ground in sunshine. In summer it is surrounded by wild grasses and flowers. In June it is ablaze with bright red poppies. Just outside the centre are five Neolithic huts, built as reconstructions of the ones excavated at Durrington Walls. From the centre it is a journey of a mile and a half to the stones. The route passes through farmland - domestic cereal crops - woodland of largely pine and hazel, beyond which are open fields where sheep and cows, the domestic descendants of aurochs graze. Travelling by shuttle bus, we may listen to the audio, chat to companions, glance out of the windows. Walking we may be more aware of the wild flowers, medicinal plants and sources of nutrition since ancient times, growing in the banks and fields. We may be watched by roe deer sheltering in the woodland or hares lying low in the open fields. We may hear the song of larks, who fly so high we cannot see them. There may be a kestrel hovering in the sky. There may be buzzards floating on a warm thermal. Flying in large flocks or on the ground are rooks, some of whom visit the stones in search of picnickers. There are the jackdaws who live in the lintels and crevices of the stones and have done for centuries. In his 'Natural History & Antiquities of Selborne', in a series of letters written following visits around the area, the famous ecologist, Gilbert White, recorded in 1788 that:

"Another very unlikely spot is made use of by daws as a place to breed in, and that is Stonehenge. These birds deposit their nests in the interstices between the upright and the impost stones of that amazing work of antiquity: which circumstance alone speaks the prodigious height of the upright stones, that they should be tall enough to secure those nests from the annoyance of shepherd-boys, who are always idling round that place."

The stones rise suddenly against the sky, waiting to be experienced.

Until such times as we can travel back in time, why Stonehenge was built and what motivated its builders remains a subject for speculation. In a world where so much knowledge is laid down for us, at Stonehenge we have space to imagine for ourselves just what it is. No-one can say we are absolutely wrong or that we are absolutely right. We cannot go and dig for evidence like the archaeologists have done in the past and may not be inclined to dig around in libraries where a great deal of archaeology is done - but we still have that most fertile of archaeological fields; that of the imagination. Whether it's a quiet day in winter or a busy day in summer, part of the experience of Stonehenge is putting down the audio and the camera and noticing how we feel in close proximity to the stones. There is something in it which resonates and gives us a connection with the universe, the planet, with nature, with one another, with ourselves - with the past, with the future, with the present moment, the eternal now.

Over a million people a year visit Stonehenge and continue to interact with it and find it a source of inspiration and fascination. People continue to celebrate the midsummer solstice in tens of thousands - 37,000 in 2014. They arrive all through the night before the solstice sunrise. From the car park, the walk is between half a mile and a mile and a half to the stones. The way goes through a field and passing a small wood, a waft of the midsummer scent of elderflowers, a sense of midsummer magic. It does not really get dark at that time of year, people pass as shadows. They come and go constantly, many of them dressed reflecting their own deep selves. Druids, witches, pagans, families, locals, tourists from a diversity of cultures and backgrounds. In the half light, a current of souls drifting by that could belong to any era - past, present, future. Shades of the past, shades of the future, the present moment. Time flows in and out of Stonehenge, it's not linear, it can go backwards, it can stand still, it can leap to the future. The shamans of the Neolithic could step out of time and touch 'the eternal now.'

People are drawn into the centre of the stones. They add their energy to the power of the stones until the whole henge pulsates with it. By dawn everyone faces the direction of the anticipated sunrise, as they have done for thousands of years. As the first sliver of sun is about to appear, people go quiet - until at the first glimpse there is a huge cheer which spreads through the watchers like a Mexican wave, an ancient response to the appearance of the sun.

The stones themselves are still, a still point in the turning world. Perhaps this is what we respond to, recognising by whatever terminology phrase our personal beliefs, in whatever era we visit, the internal and external still point of the infinite Divine. Perhaps most important is not why Stonehenge was built, or how, or what it was used for in the past but how we resonate with it and how it resonates in us. We continue to respond to and interact with Stonehenge, its appeal crosses time and cultures, whatever the intent of the builders. It speaks to us in a way we respond to - Stonehenge mirrors back what we expect to see. Although the great stones are now roped off to visitors so we can no longer touch them, Stonehenge can reach out and touch us. The 'other' Stonehenge is the one we can't see - it's inside ourselves.

For further reading

A'bury
William Stukley

An Introduction to the Archaeology
of Wiltshire
M.E. Cunnington

History of the Kings of Britain
Geoffrey of Monmouth

Inside the Neolithic Mind
David Lewis-Williams & David Pearce

Le Morte D'Arthur
Sir Thomas Mallory

Life of Merlin
Geoffrey of Monmouth

King Arthur's Place in Prehistory
- The Golden Age of Stonehenge
W.A. Cummins

Keeper of Genesis
Graham Hancock

The Ancient Secret
Flavia Anderson

The Golden Bough
James Frazer

Hamlet's Mill
Giorgio Santillana & Hertha von Dechend

Prehistoric Henges

Aubrey Burl

Stonehenge in its Landscape
20th Century Excavations
R.M.J. Cleal, K.E. Walker, R. Montague

Stonehenge and its Environs
Julian Richards

Stonehenge
Dr J.F.S. Stone

Stonehenge
Mike Parker Pearson

Sun, Moon and Wandering Stars
Mike Postins

Wiltshire Legends
L.V. Grinsell

The Stonehenge Enigma
John Bowles and Barry Brunhoff

Devizes Museum Library and the Stonehenge Galleries at Devizes Museum

Amesbury Museum

For information on visiting Stonehenge and opening hours, please see English Heritage's web site, Stonehenge.

See also:
https://www.facebook.com/StonehengeExperience/

Printed in Great Britain
by Amazon